D1234310

The
Indestructible
Crown

The Life of Albert Pick, Jr.

The Indestructible Crown

The Life of Albert Pick, Jr.

Judith Barnard

NELSON-HALL nh CHICAGO

Library of Congress Cataloging in Publication Data

Barnard, Judith.
   The indestructible crown.

   Includes index.
   1. Pick, Albert, 1895–1977. 2. Hotelkeepers—United
States—Biography. I. Title.
TX910.5.P53B37   338.7′61647940924 [B]   80–16389
ISBN O–88229–718–X

Contents

Acknowledgments

The author wishes to thank all those who gave of their time in letters and personal interviews to describe the many facets of Albert Pick, Jr. Their quotations appear throughout the book.

Albert Pick, Jr., himself, though often ill, recalled his past in weekly interviews through most of the last year of his life, providing innumerable anecdotes, insights, and philosophical ruminations for this portrait.

Corinne Pick deserves special thanks. In the background while her husband was alive, she assumed the role of raconteur and memorialist for the author after his death, and made possible the completion of the book.

Others who gave information and insight in interviews and letters were Alan Whitney, Nadine Van Sant, Alan Altheimer, Helen Mack, James Van Hook, Albert Dorfman, Chauncey Harris, Lawrence Kimpton, Jess Spirer, and Joseph Grand.

Harry Barnard, biographer and journalist, acted as consultant in this undertaking; his knowledge of American—and especially Chicago—history proved invaluable, as did his editorial criticism and support.

Foreword

How do you measure a man? His life? Obviously there are quantitative standards that are easily applied, such as height, weight, age, and net worth. In another sense, the very act of measuring implies the use of value judgments. Isaac Watts said:

> Were I so tall to reach the pole,
>   Or grasp the ocean with my span,
> I must be measured by my soul;
>   The mind's the standard of the man.

Albert Pick, Jr., was a tall man by the yardstick. He was a successful man by the gauge of business accomplishment. Yet his real stature far exceeded linear measurement, and his real success surpassed net worth. His true measure, like that proclaimed by Watts for himself, must be found in those pursuits that commanded his mind and spirit beyond devotion to mundane, practical business affairs. This is not to deride Mr. Pick's extraordinarily successful innkeeping, culminating in a nationwide chain, or the effective leadership he provided to

ix

his worldwide trade association, but his business acumen was accompanied by deep attachment to causes that transcended his day-to-day concerns with trade and commerce.

His love of people, "philanthropy" in its literal sense, turned his attention to the plight of sick children. The result was continuing support of La Rabida Children's Hospital. His abiding interest in promoting good will and understanding among nations prompted generous contributions toward international studies at the University of Chicago and the University of Miami, the People-to-People Program, and the International House in Chicago. His love of music was manifested in lasting assistance to the Ravinia Festival Association and to Northwestern University, where a handsome concert hall honors his beloved wife, Corinne Frada Pick.

His appreciation of art led him to back talented artists and musicians. He demonstrated his conviction about the value of education by establishing scholarships in music, art, and hotel training and by serving with distinction on the Board of Trustees of the University of Chicago. In fact, there was hardly any aspect of the cultural and educational life of Chicago, his birthplace, and its surrounding cities that could not claim him as an enthusiastic patron.

Thus, Mr. Pick proved, by deed, his creed that those manifestations of the human spirit—love of mankind, good will among nations, artistic expression, educational opportunity— deserved ardent nurture so that they, alive and well, could in turn minister to the needs of all of us and improve the quality of our lives.

Finally, an additional touchstone always attested to the quality of the life he led—Mr. Pick's genuine personality. It was illumined by a sense of humor that had, for its advance agent, a twinkle in his eye. His character bespoke loyalty to friends and associates. He possessed the capacity for warm and enduring friendship that blessed the lives of so many who knew him. In fact, those individuals who basked in the warmth of his friendship and those institutions that were strengthened by his philanthropy can all join in their appraisal of him by using the words of Shakespeare's Marc Anthony:

> His life was gentle, and the elements
> So mix'd in him that nature might stand up
> And say to all the world "This was a man."

Henry King Stanford, President
University of Miami

A Place in Chicago

W HEN Albert Pick, Jr., was born on July 2, 1895, his parents already had made a secure place for themselves in the vibrant city that was Chicago at the end of the century. Their son was born in the nine-room brick house given them by the boy's grandfather, Charles Pick, to start them off properly in married life, not only in a fine home, but in a fine neighborhood as well.

It was, at the time, as fine a neighborhood as a young couple could choose. The stretch of land from 20th to 45th streets on Michigan, Prairie, and Indiana Avenues was a quiet, stately enclave, with proud homes belonging to the men who were building Chicago. Traction (streetcar) magnate John Hoxie owned a quarter of the square block diagonally across the street from young Albert and Gertrude Pick at 44th and Michigan; Edward Morris, whose meat packing company rivaled Armour's and Swift's, was in the next block; and Charles Yerkes, already of almost legendary fame, lived at 32nd and Michigan.

But equally important to the newlyweds was the closeness of their own family members. Up and down the shaded streets were parents, aunts and uncles, brothers, sisters, and cousins from three large families—Pick, Frank, and Witkowsky. They were in and out of each other's homes; the children walked to school together and played together, especially on the toboggan slide made by Albert Pick to run 180 feet from the back of his lot to the stone and ironwork fence at the front.

On Friday nights, to celebrate the Sabbath, everyone was expected at Grandmother Dorshin's house. It was a commandment as firm as those in the Bible; no one was exempted. As long as she lived, Dorshin—Dorothy Witkowsky, wife of Solomon—held the strands of the family together, beginning with her own ten children and including the most "removed" cousins in the branching tree she and Solomon had planted.

They had come from Posin, Poland, in 1848, first to New York, then, in 1856, to the western frontier town of Chicago. Two of their children had been born in Europe—one of them Albert Pick, Jr.'s grandmother Pauline; eight more were born in America. The family lived on 3rd Avenue (now Plymouth Court) until the great fire of 1871 destroyed their home and their neighborhood. (They had mocked relatives who had moved to the far south side as being "countrified," but it was those relatives who provided everyone with beds when much of the city went up in smoke and flames.) After the last of the fire had been put out and the people were coming back to poke among the ruins and begin, almost immediately, to rebuild, Solomon and Dorshin took their children south of downtown to the home that would become the center of their extended family.

In that same great decade of migration, the 1840s, Jacob and Henrietta Frank came to America with two children, Isaac and Susan. Six more would be born in Chicago. In time, Isaac would marry the daughter of Solomon and Dorshin, Pauline Witkowsky, bringing the Frank family into Grandmother Dorshin's orbit.

In 1865, one year after Dorshin and Solomon moved to Chicago, a young man named Charles Pick came home from the Civil War and joined his older brother Albert in business. Incorporated in Chicago in 1857, Albert Pick and Company supplied hotels and restaurants with imported glass and china; it was the forerunner of a major supply corporation and chain of hotels, and the foundation for a fortune that, one hundred years later, in the hands of another Albert Pick, would be turned to an enriching and ennobling philanthropy.

❦

The Chicago of the 1890s—when Picks, Franks, and Witkowskys were connected by marriage and business—was a patchwork of contrasts as vivid as any in the world. It had surged up from the great fire stronger, more vibrant than ever —but tough as well: a challenging arena for those who became its giants; bleak and harsh to hundreds of thousands of others.

All of them—giants and masses alike—were drawn to Chicago by the bumptious lure of its boasts and visible accomplishments. In the weeks just after the great fire, Deacon Bross, who had lost his fortune with the burning of his newspaper, the Chicago *Tribune,* had gone east to raise capital to rebuild the city. But he was looking for more than money; he wanted people as well. "Go to Chicago now!" he had cried in New York City. "Young men, hurry there! Old men, send your sons! You will never again have such a chance to make money."

And they had come. Buying and selling, building up and tearing down, corrupting, being corrupted, exploiting, being exploited—and working to help the exploited—they came to the city on the lake, creating their own legends to match the one Chicago had long been creating for itself.

Even before the fire, the city had been a focal point of transportation, industry, and business. The brothers Charles and Albert Pick had opened their hotel and restaurant supply company in 1857 at Randolph and Wells (then called 5th Avenue, formerly an all-residential neighborhood, but just then beginning to see a few businesses move in), putting down roots in a city being called "bold, wild, amazingly strong, magnetic" by those visiting and settling there.

When the Pick brothers arrived, Chicago was boasting new waterworks (though dead fish still came through household pipes to stick in faucets or drop into bathtubs), a building boom that had tripled the value of city property in the four years from 1853 to 1856, and, in that same period, grain shipments through the Soo Canal increasing from six million to 21 million bushels a year. The iron horse, too, was changing the city, newly dubbed "Railroad King of the State"—and Illinois itself at that time had more miles of railroad track than any in the Union.

Chicago had become a convention city, with 57 hotels— eight of them first-class, as well as a literate city, with seven daily newspapers, fifteen weeklies, and six monthlies. Within two years, the city would have its first symphony orchestra, a season of grand opera, an art association, and a historical society.

And it had people. In 1857 alone, 200,000 men, women, and children surged into Chicago; and, since the increase came at a time of a national economic "panic," this added to the reputation of a city that could absorb so many new "burdens" without collapsing. "See two things in America, if nothing else," said Oxford Professor Richard Cobden. "Niagara and Chicago."

It was in this wide-open, explosive, vigorous town that Albert Pick, Jr.'s father, himself named Albert, was born to Charles and Jeanette Pick on May 17, 1869 in a walk-up apartment a block from his father's and uncle's supply company.

❦

In the twenty-six years between the birth of Albert Pick and that of his son Albert, Jr., in 1895, Chicago would see one of its greatest periods of expansion. There was, on a grand scale, the acquisition of wealth and the spending of wealth, the trade and transportation that made the city seem the spindle on which the commercial nation spun, the extended reach of arts, letters, and learning, and the growing sense among the city's giants that fortunes somehow should be returned to the people and the cities from which they sprang.

The men who made their fortunes in Chicago, transforming it as they did so, transformed it yet more in returning some of their wealth to the neighborhoods and the people who underlay it all. Their era was the last quarter of the nineteenth century, ending as Albert Pick, Jr., was born; and their deaths were symbolic: a new century, as well as a new group of business figures and public benefactors, all were born together.

It was an astonishing decade that bridged those two eras. Chicago burst with innovation and spectacle: the Columbian Exposition, the Newberry Library, and the Art Institute, all in 1893; the quiet founding of what would be the towering University of Chicago in 1892 (its neighborhood, Hyde Park, had been annexed by the city in 1889); Jane Addams' Hull House begun in 1889 and flourishing in the "other" city not visible from the steps and galleries of the Art Institute and the plush seats of Orchestra Hall; a network of water tunnels and subway lines completed in 1899–1903. The city set a building record in 1890 with 11,640 new structures costing 48 million dollars; the city was pioneering, too, in strange new buildings called "skyscrapers" talked about even across the oceans.

Before that decade, a few millionaires had left bequests to the city: Walter L. Newberry left more than $4,000,000 from his real estate dealings, half of it going to a "scholar's library"; John Crerar, railway magnate and banker, left bequests of several thousand dollars each to Presbyterian churches, orphanages, hospitals, the Historical Society, and literary societies, plus $2,000,000 for the scientific library which bears his name; Philip D. Armour established the Armour Mission with one million dollars to provide manual training for boys and girls of all creeds and races; William B. Ogden divided his bequests among Rush Medical College, the Academy of Sciences, the Astronomical Society, the University of Chicago, the Theological Seminary of the Northwest, and the Chicago Woman's Home.

And then came the decade of the passing of the giants—the transition period in which Albert Pick, Jr., was born and reached his eleventh birthday. These giants, too, left fortunes to the city's institutions; and their names bear witness to their interests and concerns: in 1897, George M. Pullman died, leaving a million dollars for a manual training school for the sons of poor men; in 1901, Philip Armour died; in 1902, Potter Palmer; in 1903, Gustavus Swift (leaving a fortune to the University of Chicago); in 1905, Charles T. Yerkes; in 1906, both Marshall Field (whose money went to the University of Chicago and the Field Museum of Natural History, among others) and William Rainey Harper, only 49 years old, who had begun "a new Baptist educational venture in Chicago"—a university with 120 of the world's greatest minds on its first faculty; it was called the University of Chicago.

And during this time, Albert Pick, Jr., and his cousins were sledding in his father's yard, walking back and forth to school, beginning to think of parties and dancing classes and travel—and becoming aware, too, of obligations: toward business, toward the community, but most of all toward family.

◊

There were six people in the Pick family at 4417 S. Michigan Avenue, plus a cook, a first floor maid, a second floor maid, and a nurse/governess. They lived in the three story house, with the four youngsters on the upper two floors; father put a ladder in his personal closet and had carpenters construct a passageway to the second floor to be used if suspicious sounds indicated rambunctiousness.

He had always been of firm, decided character and direct

action, this aggressive businessman, Albert Pick, Sr., symbolized well by the ladder going straight up to the second floor, saving time and energy over the longer, more conventional route via the stairway. He had grown up in a tough, roiling Chicago neighborhood, where gangs fought in the daylight as well as at night and boys often carried their own revolvers as they went to and from school or shops.

Albert himself carried a revolver, though he never fired it; the only time he needed a weapon in a fight, he pulled out the gun and brought it down with all his force on his opponent's head. Then, struck by an overwhelming concern that would recur many times in his life after acting hastily, he, with his brother Joe, carried the boy into their house and stood watching while their mother dressed the wound. They watched helplessly, too, while she called the police, over their objections, and then, while their mother watched, they stood again, this time through a fierce lashing from the police and the confiscation of their revolver.

It was the last event in a number that contributed to the family's move from the neighborhood which had housed both their business and their residence. They bought a house at 35th and Wabash, where they stayed through Albert's growing up.

The two brothers who began the hotel and restaurant supply company—Albert and Charles, uncle and father, respectively, of Albert Pick, Sr.—were Jews; but both had married Catholic women who insisted that the children of the marriages be raised in the Catholic faith. Jeanette Chladik Pick, Charles' wife, was especially determined that her children would be educated with a religious background, and she saw to it that Albert went off to Notre Dame for preparatory school and college. But Albert, while he accepted the religion without fuss (or much interest), was not impressed with school; he was fascinated by the world of business that his father and uncle went off to each day and that beckoned to him even as he sat in classrooms in South Bend, Indiana.

It was not that he was a failure; he was bright and could have done well, especially had he applied his own blend of determination and self-assuredness, rare in one so young. In fact, he excelled on the Notre Dame track team and in other activities where he was interested and involved. But he only really came to life in the summers when he worked for his father and uncle; and so, at the age of 16, he quit school and came to work full time at Albert Pick and Company in Chicago.

If his mother objected, she said very little. She was too busy; and, besides, she probably saw in Albert the force he would become in the business before much time had passed. It would be an attractive prospect for her—having a young, enthusiastic Albert in the business; for a long time she had been the real driving energy of the company, and she was getting tired. Jeanette Chladik, hurtled from the established, ritualized world of Carlsbad in Bohemia to the bursting city of Chicago, learning (how, she never quite knew) to run a business while managing a household and raising five children, looked at her handsome 16-year-old son and thought, Why not? Why not let him help? He seemed to have the drive and concentration her husband lacked: Charles Pick, who called himself Carl, charming, warm, extraordinarily handsome (while she herself was plain; she knew it, had always known it, but she knew, too, that she made up for it with her brains and her hard work); Charles Pick, sometime gambler whom his son Albert pursued (on orders of his mother) to local poker games in the basements of saloons to lead him home before he could drink any more or risk any more money (though he won more often than he lost); Charles Pick, who played the concertina and sang and loved to socialize (and who told tales of playing for President Lincoln and General Grant during the war); Charles Pick, who had come home from the Civil War to start the restaurant and hotel supply business with his brother Albert, found his metier as a salesman while his wife Jeanette worked several hours a day in the company offices, keeping the books, developing yearly budgets, dealing with suppliers.

Jeanette knew the family thought her taciturn and strict, especially compared with her husband; but she was overworked and overtired and had little time for the charm Charles developed in saloons and offices and living rooms. As long as the charm translated into sales, she had little argument; but she welcomed her son into the business, even though he was only 16, because she saw his potential. And, she saw his need to work.

It was a strong need: he *had* to work. He was stricter on himself than on others, this teenage boy who left the campus of Notre Dame to take his place with his father and uncle (and other businessmen he was anxious to meet and talk with) in the business world. Chicago, as a business arena, fascinated him; in business, itself, he saw the excitement and challenge of all other endeavors that, though they interested others, left him unmoved. He would grow into a difficult man in many ways— strong-willed, driving, taciturn as his mother had been—and he never mastered the ability to communicate his sense of excitement and satisfaction to others in a way that would soften the frequently severe face he showed the world (and his son). But he was a genius in his own way, and others noted it; the reputation of Albert Pick and Company grew so rapidly after he joined it that, before long, many forgot its name was that of his uncle and not of the driving young man they met in the course of daily business.

He had started at age 12, sweeping the floors and doing odd jobs; by the time he was 15, he had memorized the inventory and put in some time selling; when he left Notre Dame at 16, he began working twelve-hour days, from seven to seven, six days a week. And occasionally, on Sunday, he and his father would go to the store—their voices unconsciously hushed in the unfamiliar silence of the street, the store, the city itself, which seemed to be drowsing after the hectic pace of the week—to wrap and deliver packages to meet promised delivery dates. Their reputation around town was for reliability as much as for diversity and size of stock.

But though he worked closely with his father, and his uncle as well, the young Albert already was moving to his own inner directives; he had ideas for the company, and he was impatient with those who did not seem to have his sense of urgency. By the time he had spent ten years in the business, he was, in all respects, his own man with his own ideas.

For one thing, he had married and set up his own home in the nine-room brick house on Michigan Avenue given to him by his father. Gertrude Frank was the granddaughter of Solomon and Dorothy Witkowsky (Grandmother Dorshin who commanded attendance at her home every Friday night) and the daughter of Pauline Witkowsky and Isaac Frank.

Isaac had been brought to America by his parents when he was six. He became a merchant, like so many whom he met and lived with among those who came to America from eastern Europe. He and Pauline wandered about the midwest as he tried to find the best place for a store before they settled finally in Chicago. Their first child, Sylvia, was born when they lived on 3rd Avenue in Chicago, but their second, David, and their daughter Gertrude, were born in Omaha, Nebraska, and their other daughter, Edith, was born in Lyons, Iowa.

When, at last, in 1871, Isaac decided to return to Chicago to settle for good, the family took a house on 29th street near Cottage Grove, far from the populous (and more well-to-do) sections of Chicago. That was when Grandmother Dorshin snorted that they might as well have stayed in the country in Lyons, Iowa, if they were to live *so far* from Chicago. But that was when, too, the great fire destroyed Dorshin's home and the houses of others in the family, as well, and Isaac and Pauline were the ones who provided bed and board for burned out relatives in their "country" house.

When they did move, it was to live over Isaac's store on 22nd street near Michigan, but they soon moved to a more residential area at 27th and Michigan; and there they stayed to raise their children. It was from that house that Gertrude Frank was married in 1892 to the young, much-talked-of merchant, Albert Pick.

She was 23 years old, with a sweet, quiet face and a frail look that concealed a strong, determined will. She had been a schoolteacher and a piano and singing teacher for several years; she took on marriage with the same sense of a job to be done with which she took on all her responsibilities. Her marriage would prove to be a difficult one, and the years filled with more than their share of tragedies; but she would remain, to all who knew her, a woman of great goodness and inner fortitude who commanded deep love and a sense of caring, of wanting to protect her from all that might, in view of the past, befall her.

Her mother had died at 42 when Gertrude was 18; it was a long, brutal illness which first struck Pauline while Gertrude was away visiting relatives in Sandwich, Illinois; when she came home and saw her mother, she fainted. Her frail health and the single-mindedness of her sister Sylvia kept her from the sickroom through much of the long ordeal; Gertrude lived a good part of the next two-and-a-half years in Sandwich, while Sylvia stayed with Pauline around the clock until she died.

Then Sylvia became the companion of their father, Isaac, traveling with him and helping him in his business. In fact, Sylvia and Isaac moved in with Gertrude and Albert Pick in 1900. The house almost burst at the seams. But there was a strong sense of family that pleased everyone up and down the streets of that quiet enclave, especially Dorshin Witkowsky, who knew what *family* should mean in a harsh world.

Without warning, Isaac died in 1901. It might have been a time of withdrawal for Gertrude, who, in a short, crowded space of time had lost two parents, set up housekeeping in a large house with a demanding husband, borne three of the four children she would have, housed her sister and father, and, after her father's death, her sister and brother Dave. And there may have been a period of quiet, of protective reflection, of marking time, for, in those years, Dave married and left his sister's house in 1903. The three oldest children brought their parents the joy of beginnings to contrast with the recent sorrows of endings; the Albert Pick supply company prospered; and Gertrude became pregnant with her fourth child.

But she was doing more: she was expanding the scope of her world; she was moving outward to take note of the city that so fascinated her husband and formed the backdrop for all that they did, for their family, for their social life. There was work to be done in such a city, where the gap between rich and poor was visible and heart rending; and Gertrude Pick could no more ignore it than she could ignore the cries of her own children. With other women—many of them members of the extended family that stretched along Michigan Avenue and its neighboring streets—she began reaching out to help where she could.

The first direction she reached was toward young mothers and babies who had none of the good and comfortable things she took for granted in her own home with her own family. On September 7, 1906, the Mother's Aid Sewing Club of the Chicago Lying-In Hospital and Dispensary was created under the seal of the city of Chicago with the objectives:

> 1) to maintain one or more wards in the Chicago Lying-In Hospital to be known as the "Mother's Aid Sewing Club Ward"; 2) to provide the Institution with mothers' and babies' wearing apparel; 3) to lend assistance to poor women in the state of pregnancy; 4) to further the charitable and educational purposes of the Institution.

Among the nine founders signing the document were Gertrude Frank Pick, Ida De Lee Newman (a neighbor of Gertrude's father Isaac and sister Sylvia), Theresa Witkowsky (Gertrude's cousin) Zoe James Witkowsky (her niece), and Rose Brede, Albert Pick's sister.

It was one of many ways in which Gertrude Frank Pick would assert her individuality and maintain her personal touch with the larger world while being a wife and mother to four children—one of them, the second oldest and eldest son, being Albert Pick, Jr., whose philanthropies would include a memorial to that woman whom he remembered all his life with adoration and respect: the Gertrude Frank Pick Building of La Rabida Sanitarium.

2

Childhood

H E WAS originally named Isidore, after his father's brother who had died at 20 of a heart attack. Jeanette Pick, the mother of Isidore and Albert, Sr., wanted it that way and so it was done. But the young boy never felt comfortable with the name; and, when he was 12 and about to enter University High School (now the University of Chicago Lab School), he asked his father to let him change it to Albert, Jr. His father was pleased but, conscious of formalities, sent him to his grandparents for permission to make the change; and they, so many years after the first Isidore's death, agreed that it seemed like a good idea for the boy to carry the name of his father.

So he was Albert Pick, Jr., son, grandson—and brother, for, as warm as his relationship with his mother, and as intense with his father, the young boy's greatest affection and fiercest loyalty were reserved for his brother Laurence. He was close to his sister Pauline, a year and a half older than he, and strongly devoted to him all her life, and he would be close to Dorothy, twelve years his junior; but it was Laurence, born two years after him, who, because of his precarious health and early death, but also because of the sweetness and warmth of his personality, would stay alive within Albert with the vividness of youth even as the decades passed.

When Laurence was a child, his heart was permanently damaged in an attack of rheumatic fever. Albert, already feeling protective toward the younger brother, became his bulwark. In a real sense his whole life changed when Laurence's changed; as Laurence had to accept restrictions on his activities, so did Albert; as Laurence had to defend himself against misunderstanding, so did Albert; as Laurence was aware of the possibility of death, so was Albert. It could be fairly speculated that much of the boy Albert's later attitude toward those in need—whether emotional, cultural, or physical need—was formed during the years when he shielded Laurence from the world and learned what it was not only to have a frailty, but also to need and respond to love.

In any event, Albert became Laurence's protector, and they became each other's best friend. In the months after his illness, when Laurence was confined to bed, Albert brought him news of the neighborhood and friends and relatives; later they slept in twin beds and at night would share the world each had seen during the day, laughing together, talking in whispers, making horrendous puns, their favorite being the one about the turkeys who had eaten too many melons waddling around with "melancholy."

Looking for still other ways to express their closeness, they created a private language—a complicated arrangement of nouns punctuated by an occasional verb, all coded to specific activities, events, people, plans. The two boys refined the language until it was complex and extensive; they spoke it fluently and eventually found themselves using an occasional "secret" word in conversations with others, even in school. They kept it secret for years, even against the pleading of their well-loved sister Pauline. She called them "stubborn as mules" for keeping her shut out, so they called their private language their mule talk and used it as the verbal sign of the bond they had formed between themselves.

Laurence was not an invalid, but his list of forbidden activi-

ties was long. Dr. Mercer had cared for him when he was first
ill, coming each day in horse and buggy with two black bags—
one for instruments, one for pills—and advice on what to do
and what not to do: no strenuous exercise, no participation in
competitive games, no running up and down stairs, no undue
excitement. Laurence followed all the injunctions, and so, to
an extent, did Albert, pacing himself to his brother, as much
to make him feel less alone in his restrictions as to stay with
and protect him; it was another sign of Albert's growing reali-
zation of the needs of others and his own ability to respond to
them.

There were dozens of ways in which this was brought home
to him each day; one of the most dramatic occurred on an
ordinary day during what began as an ordinary recess.
Laurence did not look ill; for the most part, he did not act as
if he were not perfectly normal. He dressed, came to school,
did his work, went out for recess, returned to class, came home.
He differed from none of his classmates—except that, when
he went out for recess, he stood at the side, watching, rather
than participating in any sport. One day, when he was eight
years old, a basketball game was in progress, and one of the
teams was missing a player. Laurence was asked to join the
game. He shook his head. "I can't; I'm not allowed to."

"A sissy," said the basketball player, eyeing Laurence to
watch his reaction.

Laurence shook his head again. "I have a bad heart."

After a brief pause, the boy let out a bark of laughter. "Look
at the sissy; his mamma won't let her little darling play. Poor
thing. Poor sissy. Isn't it too bad?"

As if on cue, another basketball player shoved Laurence to
the ground, and Laurence, eight years old and ashamed and
frightened, began to cry. Albert was standing beside him; and
as soon as Laurence fell, he moved to stand in front of him.
"Leave him alone; he can referee or something; he can't play."
But the taunts continued; and Laurence, scrambling to his

feet, slapped the first boy on the face, at which point two of the others jumped Laurence and began to beat him up.

Albert, terrified for Laurence, lost his temper, something he did not do as easily as his father, but, when aroused, did with his father's burning anger; he socked the two of the taunting boys who had begun the fight and one who was standing in the circle around them, watching. It became a typical free-for-all, with Laurence now standing away from the flailing arms and legs as Dr. Mercer had told him to do.

Albert had a split lip and a black eye; but, to a ten-year-old, that was no reason to quit a good fight, and he was still in the middle of the fray when he noticed he had an ally, another Lawrence, this time Weiner, a small, inoffensive looking boy who attracted little attention but who was a whirling bantam cock in a fight. According to those watching he "half murdered" the boy who had tried to beat up Laurence and was turning to start in on another (or several) when two of the teachers emerged from the school, broke up the fight, and hauled Albert, Laurence, Lawrence Weiner, and his friend Lester Turner (who had done his share of "half murdering" the bullies) off to the nurse's room where they could clean up.

When the stories all were sorted out, Lawrence Weiner and Lester Turner, with Albert, became Laurence's protectors, shielding him without making him feel conspicuous, reminding him to take the pills Albert carried with him to school each day, keeping him off to the side and engaged in conversation during recess so the issue of his participating in sports never again arose.

Albert, Sr., a man who cherished a good fight and admired a good fighter, wrote to the fathers of Lawrence Weiner and Lester Turner that their sons had "the instincts of a man." There could be no higher praise from Albert Pick, Sr.

۞

In summers, the entire family—together with the families of

aunts and uncles and other neighbors in their quiet section of Chicago—went to Kennedy's summer resort on Baron Lake in Michigan. Loaded with luggage, they would take a train to Niles, Michigan, and then a horse-drawn buggy to Baron Lake, where there was an imposing hotel as well as separate cottages. The Albert Picks stayed in the hotel; but Albert, Jr., and Laurence were in and out of the cottages, too, as they made friends with other young boys staying there.

Albert, Sr., came out for weekends; the rest of the time, he worked long hours at the store, beginning his days while the sun was barely rising (since he did not have to worry about waking anyone in the empty house) and coming home late at night. But on Saturday, he would appear, bringing with him the competitive spirit that was natural to him but that also was nurtured (and had few outlets) in the daily business world.

There were swimming and tennis for everyone at Kennedy's and quiet sports such as quoits and horseshoes. There were amateur theatricals. Running and swimming races were organized by the guests themselves, while Mr. and Mrs. Kennedy and their children kept the resort clean and well-maintained.

Albert, Sr., was an exceptional athlete, challenging young men in their late teens and early twenties and beating them in such events as swimming across the mile-wide lake and back. A few years later, when he was in his early forties, Albert, Sr., challenged a young salesman in his company, a member of the German athletic club, who bragged daily of his prowess as an athlete. The two men, Albert, Sr., in tennis shoes and open-necked business shirt, the salesman in full athletic regalia, ran their race in the alley behind the Pick store, while truck and wagon drivers and everyone in the stores in the neighborhood stood and watched the contest between president and salesman of Albert Pick and Company. Albert, Sr., won by a yard, admitting to his son later that he had pushed himself as never before, since someone had to teach the salesman a lesson and there was no one else to do it. Albert never told his father—who might have found it demeaning—that there were bets on the race and a considerable amount of money changed hands; it was too bad he could not tell him, because Albert, Jr., without a moment's hesitation, had bet confidently on his father.

There were not enough challenges at Baron Lake, and soon Albert, Sr., was scouting the Illinois countryside for a site for a summer home of his own. He found it in an eighty-acre farm in Grayslake, 40 miles from Chicago, on Gages Lake. He had an old farmhouse remodeled from its stripped frame out, enlarging it in the process; and the family began spending summers there, amid other mansions, other owners who were prime movers in the buoyant Chicago business world, among them Richard Sears of the Sears, Roebuck Company, who became a close friend of Albert, Sr.

The exhilaration of designing, supervising, participating in the building of something immediately visible elated Albert, Sr.; and for many months, he was less tense in the house than his family had ever known him. Once they began using the house, there were dozens of details he had to attend to, including the fields and the garden.

The garden was special. It was one of the best parts of the summer home to Albert and Laurence who used it to launch their first business.

The garden was known far and wide for its beauty as much as its productivity—so much so, in fact, that the Scotch gardener who created it for the Pick family was stolen from them by J. Ogden Armour after Armour had been taken to view the famous garden. Armour offered the gardener not only twice whatever the Picks were paying, but a full home as well, his own car, and meals prepared and brought out to him by Armour's own cook and staff.

But before he was whisked away, the gardener gave the

Picks a marvelously lush garden with more produce than they possibly could eat themselves. So Albert, Sr., told his two sons they could sell the vegetables to the neighbors whose houses circled Gages and Rouse Lakes. Albert, Jr., at 14, already was becoming adept at taking orders from customers and delivering on time in his father's business, where he worked on weekends during the school year. He and Laurence made the rounds taking orders on Thursday and Friday; they picked the vegetables on Saturday and delivered them within an hour of picking. Their father agreed to charge them nothing for the vegetables as long as they did their own picking. He also said they could take orders for milk (the cows being as prolific as the garden), buttermilk, cottage cheese, and berries from bushes on the Pick estate.

The boys made their deliveries in their father's Pierce Arrow, which Albert, Jr., at 14, was allowed to drive. In fact, Gertrude thought her son a much better driver than his father, who tended to slide on rain-muddied roads from the ditch on one side to the ditch on the other. When the family went out together, Gertrude would not tolerate her husband's driving, but would insist on Albert, Jr., taking the wheel; it was a small but keen indication of some of the tensions that would arise later when both were capable of "taking the wheel" of Albert Pick and Company.

The Pierce Arrow would be stocked with vegetables, milk, cheese, and berries, all packed into large paper bags the two brothers bought in town each week; then off they would go on their Saturday deliveries, coming back with the day's take. Albert, Jr., when he was older, would calculate all the costs of the operation—the gardener's salary, maintaining the garden and the large Pierce Arrow—and realize he and Laurence had been running a losing business; but their father, for all his aloofness and strictness, in this as on many other occasions, was good-humored and generous and let them keep the several hundred dollars they made; in turn, the young businessmen promptly did exactly what they knew their father would appreciate: they put the money in the bank.

But that summer ended, and so did the business venture, for Albert, Sr., sold the house and its 80 acres; he had never really felt the same about the place after he lost his gardener and—so he thought—the gardens had lost their special brilliance. It was, in fact, a time of restlessness; he and Gertrude sold the house on Michigan Avenue, as well, and moved into the Del Prado Hotel on the University of Chicago campus (now the site of International House of the University), where Albert, and then Laurence, could easily walk to University High School.

One memorable year was spent in the south where Laurence could benefit from the year-round warmth. Albert, Sr.'s Uncle Albert (who, with his brother, Charles Pick, Albert, Sr.'s father, had founded the restaurant supply company that bore Uncle Albert's name) had a small cotton plantation run by tenant farmers in Citronelle, Alabama, not far from Mobile. Charles and Jeanette Pick had bought a place to be nearby, though they did not grow crops. Young Albert and Laurence spent an entire year in Citronelle; they loved the small town of 5,000 for the chance it gave them to be close to people and to the products of the earth.

In Citronelle, a daily train, known by all as "Nellie," came through each morning, taking produce to Mobile, 50 miles away. It made drop-off stops all along the way; people thus delivered and picked up goods from other towns; it was a very sophisticated kind of barter. Albert and Laurence sometimes rode the train, watching as different foodstuffs and cloth and household goods were loaded and unloaded at each stop. When they got to Mobile, they saw bananas from Central America loaded on the train, and cotton, some in bales, some already spun into thick yarn, taken off the train for the people of Mobile and for export. They also saw coffee from Central and

South America loaded on the train for delivery up and down the line; later, they would go with their grandmother to the general store to pick out the different coffee beans they would grind and blend at home.

All this gave Albert a feeling of expanse, indeed, of vastness, of people exchanging and meeting and dealing with each other on a huge stage that, he came to realize, was the whole world, accessible to him, even in Citronelle. He thought of what it meant to grow up to meet and be a part of that whole world. He thought of how his father's company—someday *his* company—could be a part of that vast world. As he looked at the bananas and coffee beans and cotton yarn, Albert clenched his fists; it was hard to wait; sometimes it was hard to be young.

Nonetheless, being young usually was being busy and content. In Citronelle, he and Laurence, when they weren't riding "Nellie" to Mobile, spent a great deal of time on the land, so different from the streets and even the grassy spaces of Chicago. They watched teams of oxen pull loads of timber and bales of cotton loaded on a flatbed truck, with the driver sitting on top of the load or running alongside cracking his whip and yelling "gee" and "haw" to keep the oxen on a relatively straight line. The two boys had never seen oxen before and watched, fascinated, as the animals heaved to pull the loads behind them, then worked easily, muscles rippling beneath the skin, as they plowed the fields just before cotton planting time.

Later, Albert would remember with a wry smile the swimming pool his great-uncle had workmen build on his property. First, the tank was built of hardwood lumber with the boards grooved tightly together. Then wells were driven to pump water into the tank, and the water began to flow. But the water seemed murky, and Albert's great-uncle, with a large dipper, brought some of it up. It was clouded with oil. "Drat it," said Albert's great-uncle. "Can't a man dig a well without getting water that's ruined by oil?" And they continued drilling, in different spots, over several months, until they found one where the water came up crystal clear, and so they had their swimming tank. Years later, telling the story, Albert, Jr., recalled how few automobiles there were at the time, that they used something call kerosene in their lamps at home, that water for irrigation was of far greater value than any oil could have been imagined to be. And he could still hear his great uncle grumbling about the nuisance of all that oil on his land!

Many years afterward, when magazines and newspapers were trumpeting the news of oil finds in and around Citronelle, an oil company representative came to Albert Pick, Jr., with a form for him to sign as the last surviving member of the branch of the family that might have a claim to the land. He signed the release but would take no money for himself, feeling he had no right to it—the land had been parceled out to other cousins over the years, and he had never been given any of it; he signed over the $10,000 release payment to La Rabida Hospital, of which he was then chairman of the board.

❧

Albert and Laurence went through grammar school together and then to the University High School. By this time, the family had moved to the Del Prado Hotel, where they had a large apartment with maid service; Gertrude Pick brought her own linens, not liking to use the hotel's. Laurence and Albert walked to school together as they had walked to Forestville Grammar School, dressed against the cold winters in high boots, overshoes, leggings over all, mufflers, and heavy coats. When the weather was too bad for Laurence to chance the walk, they were driven in the family's horse-drawn carriage.

But Laurence stayed only two years in high school; he transferred as soon as his father would let him to the school of the Art Institute of Chicago.

Enforced rest, or inclination, or both, led Laurence to art.

He studied drawing, painting, and design at the Art Institute but found his real bent in the design and creation of women's clothes. In days long before wealthy women went to department stores or bought ready-to-wear, Laurence was designing some of the most innovative garments to be found anywhere for women who had all their clothes made to order. His combinations of fabrics, cut, and style attracted wide attention; and it was not long before he decided he wanted to be a dress designer with his own couturier shop in Chicago.

Albert backed him, as he backed him in all things, though when their father insisted that Laurence work for Albert Pick and Company as a salesman, Albert backed his father, at least for a time. He urged Laurence to give it a try; if there was anything that Albert felt about as strongly as he felt about Laurence, it was the family business, *his* business, where he would succeed—he knew this already—far beyond the point his father and uncle had reached. It was a driving need in him to go as far as possible, to create new horizons in the company (and eventually in other areas, as well, through philanthropy); and he wanted Laurence there with him. So he urged him to come to work.

As an experiment, it failed; and Albert was the first to know it. Laurence was miserable and angry and exceedingly tense. Albert took it upon himself to go to their father and ask him to find something else for Laurence; it was not, at that point, a question of his health but of his emotional well-being, which, Albert pointed out to his father, could affect Laurence's physical health.

Gertrude Pick, herself not overly strong, her heart sometimes thumping in irregular rhythms that frightened her, thought Laurence should do as he pleased; she wore the clothes he made (as did most of her friends) and would have been satisfied to have him become a dress designer.

Albert, Sr., compromised. His son was not going to open a couturier shop bearing the Pick name in Chicago, but he could work at something more artistic than hotel equipment if he wanted. The father bought Burley and Company, a competitor in hotel china and glassware, but better known for a retail store on North Wabash with imported crystal, china, linens, and objects d'art.

In fact, Albert, Sr., did not buy the company "for" Laurence. He bought it because of another of its activities: it was a major supplier to railroads. Albert, Sr., wanted that business because it reached lines that ran from coast to coast; originally, he had planned to liquidate the retail store on Wabash Avenue as soon as he bought it and concentrate on the whole-sale business, merging part of Burley's with his own supply company and expanding the railroad division, perhaps as a subsidiary of Albert Pick and Company. However, he liked the manager of the retail store, and, when he was looking for something "artistic" for Laurence to do, he sent him there for training as an assistant manager.

Laurence, then in his 20s, loved Burley's from the first day; and, although there was some more desultory talk of a couturier business, with Albert, Jr., as his partner to handle finances and distribution, he was more and more content to work at designing table settings to show off the merchandise, some of which ran as high as $10,000 for a dozen service plates. He became very successful, especially in dealing with wealthy residents of Chicago and its suburbs, often going to their homes to set up a dining table for a dinner party of twenty-five or more and then selling the customer the entire service, plus the imported linens, candle holders, napkin rings, and centerpiece. After one such sale, the biggest in Burley's history, Laurence, elated, asked his father to come to the store. (His father had never done so; compared to the wholesale end, it was insignificant, and Albert, Sr., did not waste his time on small matters.) He did come, with his brother-in-law David Frank, who also worked in the business, and was sufficiently impressed with the size of the order, and its value, to compliment Laurence on his feat. It was something Laurence, and Albert, Jr., never forgot; compliments from their father were so rare that each rested like a jewel in a separate setting to be treasured and taken out to be admired when grimmer times followed—as inevitably they did.

But before those days at Burley's, Albert and Laurence spent years as schoolmates, best friends, and confidants. And it was to Laurence that Albert confided the disappointments and joys of those passing years.

3

College and Romance

ALBERT'S classmates at University High School were divided into two groups: those who wanted to go to the University of Chicago and those who wanted to go to Cornell. Albert was in the latter group, a large one, in which were most of his friends and most of the track and football stars whom he admired. He, himself, had run in track meets in high school and played a little football. He was best at track—in fact, he and his sister Pauline often raced each other neck and neck, both being swift and long-winded; they beat everyone in the neighborhood no matter where or how long the race, and then they would come home and race each other.

But his father had his own plans. When Albert, Jr., approached his father with his wish to go to Cornell, Albert, Sr., told him that he was already enrolled at the University of Chicago, with his deposit paid, that he would live at home (in a huge twelve-room apartment at 5300 Hyde Park Boulevard to which they would move shortly so that he could be within walking distance of the campus), and that he would continue to be the strong supporter of Laurence that he had been ever since Laurence was a child.

Storms may have threatened; surely there was electricity in

the air; but Albert knew he could not prevail against his father. He was very angry, and disappointed, but his father had presented him with a *fait accompli,* and he was learning to bend where necessary and stand firm where there was hope of accomplishment. He had watched his father take the independent step he himself longed for by buying out his (Albert, Sr.'s) father and uncle, taking over the family supply company: he had watched his father take charge of the 160 acres bought by his cousins (Uncle Albert's children) and develop them as the village of Villa Park, Illinois; and he was beginning to believe there was nothing his father could not do and could not make profitable. When he could look at his father judiciously, Albert could call him imaginative and strong, a superb merchant, a man of good taste. When caught up in one of their almost constant struggles, he called him a martinet, a powerful, determined, sometimes irrational, difficult man. They were all the same person, but Albert must often have felt there were several Albert Pick, Srs., all exerting pressure on him to live and work according to dictates over which he had little control.

In any event, he went to the University of Chicago and did well in his class work. He joined the track team with great enthusiasm but never excelled as he had thought he might when in high school; the competition was tough and his build was slight, too slight to make up for it with doggedness.

Too slight, as well, for the football team; Coach Stagg (after whom the university's athletic field would be named) tossed him out of the locker room "in 30 seconds," as he later recalled demanding to know what he was doing there. "We have no room," Stagg said, "for substitutes from high school. These guys'll kill you."

He loved the track team, however, and its scheduled meets at other campuses. It was no longer necessary for his own security that he win, or even win a letter. He was losing his shyness and gaining that special aura that athletes wear as they walk about a campus.

His father never came to a meet, which disturbed him, but he never brought it up in their conversations; instead, he developed his own compensations. He and Laurence were still close, as adults, now, instead of children; and they gained strength from each other. They spent long hours in talk and at play. At vacation times or on weekends, they would go to formal dress parties, come home at two or three in the morning to change clothes, then drive out to the golf course and line up their clubs, waiting for sunrise. After nine holes, they were home in time for breakfast with the family and then, at last, to bed.

Albert was close, too, to Pauline and fond in a big-brother way of Dorothy, twelve years younger than he. He was aware that it was Dorothy who had won a special place in their father's heart; she was the brightest of them all, father would say, and he would unbend with her as with none of the rest of them, even his wife whom he adored.

But Albert, except for his closeness to Laurence and the protective love he felt toward his mother (who, like Laurence, made light of her fragility and thus commanded even more concern from those around her), was turning more and more to himself for confidence, to his activities at the university and his plans for the future with his father's company.

An incident at the university would burn bright in his memory for the rest of his life; it gave evidence of the kind of man he would be. He had been studying a wide variety of subjects, curious about many, feeling duty-bound to take others to prepare himself for business. (In fact, his father encouraged him to take a heavy load of subjects and expected him to do well; he even offered him $1,000 if he made Phi Beta Kappa.) His list of subjects included every course he could take in economics, money and banking, and corporation finance, all in the School of Business Administration. He became friends with the professors and would meet with them after class to discuss problems or questions he had gathered when listening to his father or working part-time in the business. He took, as well, accounting, anthropology, German and French, ancient and medieval history, and a number of courses in literature.

But he also sought out extracurricular activities, his favorites, after the track team, being sportswriter for the university's daily "Maroon," and the Blackfriar's, a club for amateur theatricals. Soon Blackfriar's was taking more and more of his time in evening and late-night rehearsals; it was becoming a chore to get up early and meet his Public Speaking class. So, often he did not, sleeping through until he had to go to chapel (mandatory for everyone) at 10 a.m.

Warned by Professor Nelson that he would be failed if he continued to miss class, Albert, ordering his own priorities, continued with late rehearsals and continued as well to miss class—and was failed by Professor Nelson.

A failure at the University of Chicago made a student ineligible for all university competition, which meant no more track or basketball for Albert. Furious, he went to the department head, who, learning that Albert would have received an "A" had he not cut so many classes, tried to convince the professor to give him a "C." But Professor Nelson, insulted by his student's willfulness and the blatant way he had been ignored, was adamant.

All other recourse failed. Even the great professor James Weber Linn attempted to intervene on Albert's behalf ("Albert you shouldn't have done it," he said, and Albert agreed: "I should receive some punishment but this is going too far."); but Professor Nelson, even before a man he admired above all others, would not be moved. So the failure was emblazoned on Albert's record. And immediately he registered for the next semester of Public Speaking, taught, as the first, by Professor Nelson.

Throughout that second semester, Albert's speeches in class were all variations on a single theme: the smallness and audacity of a professor who would take it into his own hands to determine a student's future, the lack of flexibility, the blindness to possibilities of cooperation between teacher and student, the total failure to understand another human being. The speeches followed one another inexorably, their rolling phrases, describing the unnamed professor, ending always with the promise that the professor would be named when the time came.

Halfway through the semester, Professor Nelson privately apologized to Albert and invited him for a beer and conversation on the subjects of college life and problems peculiar to professors and to students. He also asked Albert to apologize for the glacial speeches with which he had filled his class speaking obligations. Albert refused, saying it gave him satisfaction to see Professor Nelson upset. In fact, he added, he was thinking of taking the third semester of Public Speaking, again with Professor Nelson.

Eventually, the two men had their beer and their conversation and became good friends. Albert received top grades for Public Speaking that semester and the following, when he did take it again. But that steely quality which led him on from speech to speech, each one laced with drama and suspense and scorn for the unnamed professor, would be seen many times in the business world, and later in the philanthropic one in which he would see that his money was used in the ways he thought best toward the ends he thought best and by the people he determined to be the best. His father, too, would one day see that quality in his son and would know how much of it came from him.

❦

The business was waiting when he graduated from college. It had changed and grown since the early days when Albert and Charles Pick, home from the Civil War, had set up their shop and delivery service on Randolph Street. Now the two founders owned a small antique shop on Michigan Avenue, their shares in the business bought out by Charles' son Albert, who, to raise the necessary money, had brought in three of his brothers as joint owners with him. Besides the store, the new owners had launched a catalogue business providing domestic and imported supplies for hotels, restaurants, and bars.

The original small shop had long ago been swallowed up by an imposing cluster of buildings that served as display space, warehouse, and sales mart combined. The Victorian buildings, with windows trimmed with ornamental stone and crisscrossed by a maze of fire escapes, were rented by Albert, Sr., and his brothers and later modernized by them with plate glass windows and a metal canopy which blazoned "Albert Pick and Company" as boldly as any of them had ever dreamed. The interiors had been remodeled as well, and the spacious display areas had become the unofficial headquarters for cooks, chefs, waiters, bartenders, hotel and club managers, and others in allied businesses who came in during their off-hours; not only could they browse through row after row of china, glass, silver, kitchen utensils, dishwashers, appliances, bowling supplies, linens, and hundreds of other items they used in their daily work, they also mingled with salesmen who could give immediate information on equipment (and take orders at the same time). Equally important, Albert Pick and Company became a kind of employment mart where job seekers and employers could meet and have quiet talks and make their arrangements without attracting attention. In all, by 1910, the company was one of the best known in the city, respected and used by everyone in all branches of the hotel, restaurant, and saloon businesses.

In 1912, Albert, Sr., built his own warehouse at 1200 West 35th Street in an area that would become densely packed with light and heavy industry. The building had five stories and a full basement—48,000 square feet in all. The offices and showroom remained at the old site on Randolph Street.

It was a major step for the still young owner—but he was

building not only for himself, but for others as well: the relatives who continually came to him for jobs and, most important, his son, at the time beginning his studies at the University of Chicago and working during the summers in his father's company.

Both men, Albert, Sr., and Albert, Jr., had the same attitude toward business. There were tensions between them that would explode on many occasions, but they were tensions of personality and individual ways of doing business rather than general goals and ideals. Both believed in hard work; both believed in applying the same strict injunctions to themselves that they applied to others; both believed in business as an endeavor worthy of a man's best efforts and talents. And both believed in philanthropy, though it was the son who would add that aura to the Pick name.

So when Albert, Jr., began to work in the company on weekends and summer vacations, he pushed himself as his father did and learned the functions of each department as if that were where he would spend his working life. He never questioned the need for working as he did, as he never questioned working for his father's company; there were certain patterns to his life, and the idea of work and this special company were part of them.

Other patterns in his life gave evidence of changing when he was eighteen, though he was not to realize it for some time. As Albert, Jr., was studying at the University of Chicago, socializing with his friends in the Reynolds Club, acting with the Blackfriar's, and running on the track team (until Public Speaking ended that activity), a thirteen-year-old girl was making her concert debut as a pianist with the San Francisco Symphony Orchestra. Later, she played with the Seattle Symphony and, in the next few years, with other orchestras in cities up and down the west coast. In the audience for one of the concerts was Dr. Glen Dillard Gunn, music critic for the Chicago *Herald and Examiner* and director of his own music school in Chicago. Backstage, Gunn told the young girl's mother he would give her daughter a full scholarship to come to Chicago and study with him; she had before her, he said, a remarkable career.

It was one of those confluences of events that change people's lives from far-off beginnings. When Gunn made his offer, Corinne Frada was fifteen years old, a child prodigy who thought she wanted only to be a concert pianist; her mother encouraged her, traveling with her to her concerts, carrying her luggage and her practice keyboard for use on trains and in hotels. Her mother also had a sister in Chicago, Mrs. Elijah N. Zoline, who said she would be delighted to give Corinne a home while she studied with Dr. Gunn. Orinn Zoline, Corinne's cousin, was a fraternity brother of Albert Pick, Jr.

It was a tiny, very lovely young girl who came to Chicago in 1913 to study with Dr. Gunn. She was poised and seemed older than her age, but she was shy; her schedule of private tutoring in high school subjects, and six hours a day of practice, kept her largely isolated from people her own age. In Albert Pick and his sister Pauline and brother Laurence, she found a family —friends who could share her gaiety and need for fun but also could understand the rigorous demands of her kind of life.

But there was more than "family feeling" in the group of friends. Albert, Jr., was enormously impressed with the vivacious young girl who showed a dedication and seriousness he had not seen in his partners in dancing class when he and they were fifteen; nor, though he saw plenty of serious students, was he so attracted by any of the girls at the University.

There was nothing formal or planned—Corinne was, after all, but fifteen years old and working toward a lifetime career —but the two found themselves spending a great deal of their free time together and discovering how many ideas they shared. It may be that Albert even found a roundabout way to link the two of them even more closely by telling Corinne of his great uncle Conrad Witkowsky, who went west in the great gold rush of the early 1850s, leaving behind in Chicago his thirteen-year-old fiancee, Pauline. She sent him, by Pony Express, long, elegantly penned letters describing the Lincoln-Douglas debates, the coming election, and the busyness of her days in the bustling city of Chicago. Conrad kept every letter, coming back ten years later to marry the faithful Pauline in 1864. Albert had seen a few of those same letters, saved by his cousin Alan Whitney (once Witkowsky) and eventually given to the Chicago Historical Society.

In any event, the two young people found much to talk about; and those quiet months were of great importance to them, coming as they did as an island in time before the outbreak of war and the wrenching change it made in everyone's lives.

4

Corinne

THE United States entered the First World War in the spring of 1917; within a few months, an officers' training camp was opened at Fort Sheridan, north of Chicago. Young men in their senior year of college were invited to join the officers' training class and receive their commission after a brief, intensive indoctrination. With some of his friends, Albert Pick, Jr., responded to the invitation and signed up with the first class at Fort Sheridan.

His father, when told about it the next evening, was angry. It is probable that a significant factor in his anger was his son's independence of action, regardless of the act itself; but in addition, he was convinced that any dramatic change in their family structure would endanger the fragile health of his wife and Laurence. So he put his foot down: Albert was not going to join the army; he was not going to train to become a commissioned officer. If Albert wanted to help the war effort, he already was in the best possible position: Albert Pick and Company was in the business of supplying Army cantonments and hospitals with equipment, linens, appliances, and other items they needed; Albert, Jr., would take charge of the liaison work between the quartermaster corps (army camps), the sanitary corps (army hospitals), and the supply company itself. In effect, he would be working for the government.

Albert objected, but he was trapped by his own concern for his mother and brother. He knew Gertrude had high blood pressure and heart trouble—the family talked about it often and took care of her as if she already had become the invalid she might become if they were incautious—and, of course, for most of his life he had acted as Laurence's protector and companion. In addition, Dr. Black had said that sudden change and shocks could be fatal to Gertrude Pick. Against that, there was nothing much a young man could do; to proclaim his desire to move away from those who needed him and place his life in danger, thus giving them constant concern and fear, simply because he felt impelled (as did his classmates and all his friends) to help America in its need, could be seen, given all the arguments, as selfishness and immaturity, especially since there were other ways he could help his country.

Albert, Sr., working swiftly after his son's capitulation, spoke to several men he knew in the Federal and local governments, and, within a couple of weeks, could show his son the official papers granting him an exemption from military service based on civilian work which was crucial to the war effort. It had been a masterpiece of cutting through bureaucracy; and even Albert, Jr., was impressed. But his father waved it aside and told him to get on with his work, to ignore the retail and wholesale responsibilities he had been ready to assume with Albert Pick and Company, and to devote himself to the United States Army.

It was the second time Albert had been prevented from leaving home and making his own way, but working for the quartermaster and sanitary corps was far different from going to the university; in a real sense, he did leave home, spending his days with people, and in situations, far from those so long familiar to him. The rhythm of his life was changed; his circle was enlarged; his knowledge of the world expanded, satisfying curiosities and hungers he did not even know were within him. Much of what he did with his later life had its beginnings here, in a greater understanding of people and the pressures that move them. (Later, when he was drafted, all these new understandings were greatly expanded again; but the real beginning was the sudden break with the familiar routine of home and a world bounded in large measure by the will of his father.)

Chicago, too, went through a period of change with the war. In the years just before it, William Burnham had put forth his comprehensive development plan—an attempt to create order in the hectic pace of building up, tearing down, cutting new streets, filling in land, and generally rearranging the lake shore and the inland face of the city. Traffic jams choked every street and every intersection; the population was growing visibly, by the thousands, the tens of thousands, with slums and mansions springing up almost overnight, drawing invisible lines beyond which whole groups of people might not go.

Those were years of tension and explosive ideas; the Industrial Workers of the World were headquartered in Chicago; the city had nearly half a million German-born citizens and equally large numbers of other nationalities, many of them working in despicable conditions in ill-paying jobs and housed in confined areas, tumbled together tightly with "their own kind." The real turmoil, which itself would be a forecast of much more to come, would occur later, after the war, in the riots of July 1919; but there was trouble rumbling beneath the surface long before that, and those working in the heart of the city knew it. Jane Addams knew it; she was teaching skills for survival and for jobs at Hull House, and she told others there were bad times ahead. William Hale Thompson, running for mayor against Robert Sweitzer, may have known it; but he ignored the signs and kept his campaign at high pitch, as if re-election was all that mattered, courting the "alien" vote and giving speeches that fit the appellation of "Big Bill."

And in Europe a war began.

By the time Woodrow Wilson went before Congress asking them to help him send America to war, Thompson had been elected Chicago's mayor, surprising many by his immediate "reform" of closing all saloons on Sunday; and because of Jane Addams and another Chicagoan named Julian W. Mack, the first juvenile court in America had been established in Chicago. The city was moving, growing, spurting out in dozens of directions with beauty, with violence, with poverty, with wealth. And in the midst of it all, America went to war— and Chicago held its breath, to see how its German and other "alien" citizens would react.

Riots had been predicted; none came. Instead, aldermen and other city officials joined with university professors and businessmen to come out officially for universal military training; owners of yachts (including the mayor) entered their boats for a flotilla of sub-chasers; the Chicago chapter of the Red Cross was formed and became one of the biggest money raisers in the city's history; the Pullman plant began making cannon shells; garment factories turned out over $3,000,000 worth of uniforms for the military; the McCormick reaper works converted to the manufacture of machine guns and ammunition wagons; recruiting banners and American flags flew in great colorful clouds above State Street and Michigan Avenue; Mrs. J. Ogden Armour and many of her friends said they would trim their household budgets to help the war effort; and, when food was rationed, restaurants put up signs to ease the pain, such as the one that said, "Use only one lump and stir like hell—we won't mind the noise." So Chicago put aside its street-widening and lake-filling; it had a war to fight, and all dissenting voices were drowned out in patriotic activity.

Albert Pick, Jr., did not think in terms of "popular" or "unpopular." He and his friends at the University of Chicago thought the war was necessary; and when his father talked him into staying at home and working with the supplying of the armed forces, he turned all his energies into doing *that* necessary thing. Corinne had gone back to her home in Seattle. They were corresponding regularly; and, between his family responsibilities, his correspondence, and his job, he had little time for a social life more extensive than an evening out with friends now and then. So he had the time and the will to turn his job into something far more, in all likelihood, than his father had envisioned.

In fact, within a short time, he became almost indispensable to General Kniskern, who was in charge of the quartermaster depot on 39th Street. The two men had worked out the basic system of rotation by which various cantonments were to be furnished equipment; and, when it was working smoothly, the General, impressed with the young man and liking him personally, as well, offered him the job of his assistant with the rank of Captain. "Your exemption will run out one of these days, Albert," he said. "I'm an old army man, and I know how these things work. Somebody will look at it and decide it ought to be recalled, and you'll be up for the draft—as a private, Albert—overnight. So you're better off taking this: a captaincy, a job with me; you can live at home, but you'll be a uniformed captain. Lots of advantages in that."

Albert liked the idea. He liked the General, and he was able to look on his work as necessary to the war effort. In addition, he was still spending a good bit of time with Laurence, who was stronger in these years than ever before, and he was able to see that his mother was more comfortable knowing where he was and what he was doing. (As Thomas Wolfe would write one day, the war fever infected everyone in the early days, and Gertrude felt it, too; it made her shiver with apprehension. She could imagine Albert killed a dozen ways, while the rest of the world cheered on the opposing forces. No, it was far better to have Albert in Chicago, living at home, cared for, caring for others.)

But again, his father said no. The reasons were more obscure this time. There seems to have been a feeling in Albert, Sr., that he had controlled events this far and would continue to do so, that he would not have his son in the army, subject to others' whims and dictates, and that he would generally oppose any changes in the current state of affairs unless he himself initiated them.

It was a demonstration of nearsightedness that Albert, Sr., would show few times (though those would be crucial ones) in his life. In this case, it left his son open to the draft, as the General had predicted, and altered not a few, but most, of his father's ideas. What was perhaps even more bitter for him to take later was that Albert, Jr., had been offered a second chance to avoid the draft—as a captain on the staff of a magazine called "The Modern Hospital," owned by Colonel Hornsby of the sanitary corps; the Colonel himself offered Albert the position, but again his father refused to allow it.

It was only a few months before the notice of reclassification came from the draft board, and all requests and demands made to the authorities by Albert, Sr., were turned away as, this time, impossible to grant. So, too, did General Kniskern refuse Albert, Jr.'s request for the original offer of captain on his staff; the work was done, he said, as did, later, Colonel Hornsby. Albert, Jr., had ninety days to prepare for the life of a private in the United States Army.

❧

His mother was not told; Pauline and Dorothy and Laurence knew. Pauline, closer to him than the others, secretly wrote to Corinne, asking her to come for a visit, to stay at their home. It was October, 1917.

Corinne was changed—older, more assured, a nineteen-year-old professional who toured to play with symphony orchestras and was confident of the impression she made when she came into a room, sure of her loveliness and easy grace with strangers; yet she was astonishingly the same in her warmth and affection and the comfortable way she fit into the family

as if the years of separation had never been. Albert, Jr., whose
social life had always been fairly limited and whose knowledge
of the world was less sophisticated than hers, was as impressed
with her poise as with her delicate beauty.

But there was surely more to the speed with which he made
sure she would be his before he was drafted: most likely, he
saw in Corinne Frada the same combination of steel and femi-
ninity he saw in his mother. Corinne, though slender, was more
sturdy, physically, than Gertrude Pick, but she showed the same
willingness to cleave to a man that Gertrude had shown. And
though Albert had vowed many times to himself that he would
do nothing to cause her pain, as his father often did to his
mother, he must have sensed that, if pain or trouble were to
come to a marriage, from whatever source, it could only be a
measure of satisfaction to a man to know he would have a
strong woman at his side—one who would stay at his side.

There was something else, too. The disappointment of being
prevented from going to Cornell had not fully faded when Albert had been prevented from other steps—joining officers'
training and taking one of two highly desirable positions with
the army, positions of status and responsibility. However much
he was moving in new groups of people, however much he had
felt himself necessary to the war effort, he still was following
paths marked out by his father, living in his father's house,
eating at his father's table. There must have been a driving
need at this time to establish himself as a man in his own right.
The draft was not sufficient to achieve what he needed
(though, as it turned out, his experiences once he was in the
army went far toward helping him prove himself to himself
in ways his work at the company, and as liaison with the
army, had not done).

In any event, as soon as he acknowledged to himself that
he was in love with this stunning girl from Seattle—who also
had deep affection from his brother Laurence and his sister
Pauline (added approval that could only help!)—he was in-

tensely impatient. He waited only long enough to set the stage properly—a touch of drama he would employ again and again in connection with business and philanthropy—by borrowing his mother's Rough and Lang electric car (35 miles per hour and a range of 75 miles on one charge of the batteries) and taking Corinne to dinner and the theater.

For her part, Corinne saw a young man with a strong, handsome face and pleasing manner that drew others to him quickly and firmly. Already, there was evidence of the ways in which future years would bring strong friends who would have affection for him (and as great affection for his wife) and praise, not only for his business acumen, but for his worth as a man who cared about others.

Much of this Corinne could predict from knowing him, personally and through his letters. The Albert Pick, Jr., she sat beside in his mother's electric car that night in 1917 was more sophisticated than he himself thought, with a sweetness and shyness that endeared him to her, combined with a sharp wit, occasionally caustic when it hit on others' foibles, and a sense of the world—its order, its necessities, its attractions—that appealed strongly to her at this time.

She had been touring widely, practicing her piano when not actually giving concerts, spending long hours traveling with her mother, who tended to organize her hours as well as her days. The thought of a life with Albert, sharing his world and helping him build it, teased at her the more she thought of it. The days she was a guest in his home convinced her that this was where she wanted to be, at Albert's side, with Laurence, Pauline, and Dorothy as part of her family, creating a home. Whatever drive she had had to be a concert pianist (and at one time it had been very strong, though owing much to her mother) faded before the strength, and the needs, of Albert Pick, Jr.; and Corinne knew she wanted to marry him.

Many years later, she would say they "proposed to each other" in the car that night, on the way home from the theater.

Albert would remember he parked under a street light and launched himself into a speech about love and the search for it and what her loveliness meant to him, while Corinne, in a sort of chorus background, murmured, whenever he paused, "yes, yes, go on," finally bringing him to the end of his speech by asking outright if he was proposing to her.

So perhaps they did propose to each other. However it was done, they sat under the street light vowing their love and, as well, a patently impossible promise: that they would keep the events of the evening secret until the proper time came to announce their engagement to the family.

It took about fifteen minutes for the news to be made public: Albert to his brother in the room they shared, Corinne to Pauline in the room they shared. And then the four of them went in to wake Albert, Sr., and Gertrude and tell them the news.

The biggest hurdle was Corinne's mother. The young people had decided not to wait until Albert was called up by the army and completed his tour of duty. They set the date a month hence, on December 27, 1917, Albert's parents' 25th anniversary; and Corinne wrote to her mother, describing in careful detail her feelings for Albert and her decision to give up the idea of a career as a pianist. She wanted, she told her mother, a normal life with a husband and a family and a home; she wanted no more of the endless traveling and pressures of concertizing. Finally, she said she was going to wait in Chicago for Albert to return from the army. She was not, in other words, planning to go home again, except for some vague time in the future when she would come as a visitor—a married woman with her husband.

There was silence from Seattle, and there was silence after each of the three telegrams Corinne sent, following the unanswered letter. A fourth telegram, insisting on a response, brought one: her mother was coming to Chicago to talk Corinne out of this absurd idea.

It was a difficult time. Her mother was adamant, but so was Corinne—two strong-willed women who knew exactly what they wanted. Albert was jumpy, expecting to hear each day that he had to report to camp. His mother was warm to Corinne, cool to Corinne's mother, while trying to make plans for the wedding. Albert, Sr., suffered, in an odd way, perhaps most of all: here, under his roof, was a woman arguing against an action which he approved; more, she *knew* he approved it. Such opposition, especially in his own home, had never arisen; had it done so, it would have been squelched as totally unacceptable. But here it was, and there was nothing he could do about it.

In fact, Albert, Sr.'s silent support gave his son additional confidence; and that, plus Corinne's strength, prevailed, even over the last-ditch proposal by her mother that the two go ahead and get married if they were so sure that was what they wanted, and then Corinne would resume her career, with her mother as manager, living with the young couple when Corinne was not on the road. It did not work, nor did her final despairing cry that Corinne hadn't the faintest idea how to keep house and she—her mother—could keep house for them at the same time she was Corinne's manager.

Corinne and Albert must have recognized the desperation in these pronouncements—the terrible fear of a woman about to lose the career she had hoped to experience vicariously through her daughter; but, in their youth and their absorption with each other, they were able to stand firm without regrets for others' anxieties. And so they were married.

They were married on Albert's parents' anniversary, in the Standard Club, then at 23rd and Michigan Avenue. The club, almost 50 years old at the time (the first building had burned down in the great fire), had been the scene of parties and dancing classes for Albert, Jr., and his cousins through the years of their growing up. It was the Jewish counterpart of the Chicago Club (which banned Jews from membership) and had an elegance that, combined with its tradition of social service, gave its members a sense of identity as well as pride, both in themselves and in their city.

Pauline was Corinne's bridesmaid; Laurence was Albert's best man. It was a large wedding, with out-of-town guests and all the relatives of the three extended families and their friends. But the focus of the wedding was the young couple and, more narrowly, it was Corinne's wedding dress, designed and made by Laurence, who had worked for a month on the yards of heavy satin, all hand embroidered. Setting off Corinne's delicate features and dark wavy hair, it was magnificent; and even Albert, Sr., who had called Laurence a "sissy" for spending his time at painting and embroidery and needlepoint, took pride in his son's creation that drew such praise from the guests.

And then the newlyweds went to the Blackstone Hotel in downtown Chicago for their wedding night—where Albert, opening his suitcase, found neatly folded a flaming pink silk nightshirt that his mother had bought for him at Marshall Field's and that Laurence, who did his packing, had put on top so it would be the first thing he and Corinne saw.

They took a short trip to Texas for their honeymoon, but their time together was brief; shortly after they returned to Chicago, Albert was called up by the army and told to report to Camp Grant in Rockford, Illinois. Within a few days, he was boarding a troop train, leaving his weeping mother and ramrod-straight father on the platform with his bride—small, dry-eyed Corinne, alone in Chicago except for his family, letting him go with a small smile and a kiss and not telling him, even in a whisper as he held her, that she was afraid for him and uncertain of the future.

So Albert went off to the army in January 1918, as Europe was being torn apart and America, brave and confident, sent hundreds of thousands of her sons to make the world safe for democracy.

5

The War

IN THE winter of 1918, Camp Grant recorded one of the greatest snowstorms in its history, with some of the lowest temperatures. Albert's company lived in wooden barracks perched on stilts to keep rain and snow from seeping in; still, they were colder than any of them could remember. They were dressed in ill-fitting uniforms and shoes. Sweaters, coats, and blankets were in short supply. Their only heat in the barracks came from a couple of pot-bellied stoves that warmed the first two rows of those who huddled close, but left the others in the cold. Their most notable victory over the weather was in the digging of tunnels through high banks of snow from one barracks to another; crouched low, the men could traverse much of the camp without walking in the subzero wind.

It was all new for Albert—the surroundings, the people with whom he ate and slept and trained, the rigid, often unexplained, rules, the discomfort, the routine of each day. In some ways, however, things were the same: he managed to be better cared for than many of his companions, and later this would cause him some trouble.

At first, there were no problems; he was well-liked, and there was little jealousy when his father and mother made sure their son would be warm. They sent extra blankets (though these were pulled off in the middle of the freezing nights by teeth-chattering soldiers in other bunks in the barracks), as well as uniforms ordered from Marshall Field and Company in Chicago, wrap-around puttees, and army-type shoes made by a shoemaker who had Albert's last.

There may have been some joshing at "the swell" whose parents supplied him where the army failed to do so, but none of it was antagonistic: Albert marched with the best of them in rain and snow and freezing sleet; he groused with them over blistered feet; he did well though not spectacularly on the rifle range, scoring as third-ranked marksman rather than second-ranked sharpshooter or first-ranked expert; and he shared the load of keeping the barracks spotless for sudden inspections.

But there were differences between his background and that of the other men, differences that influenced the course of his army experience. One such difference was the kind of social milieu from which he came to the army. This was brought home to him one day when his barracks was being inspected by a major who had not been there before but was known for his strict application of regulations.

Albert, with the rest of the company, was at attention, looking straight ahead, when the major, a large, handsome man, moved into Albert's field of vision and Albert found himself looking at Hays McFarland, friend from the University of Chicago, companion in countless games of billiards, pool, bowling, and poker. McFarland stopped in front of him, impeccable and impassive, and Albert blurted out, "Well, for the love of God, look who's the major!"

His words fell into an astonished silence; then the top sergeant called him out of ranks for insubordination. Later, as predicted, he was ordered to the major's office for punishment, where the differences surfaced again.

McFarland burst out laughing when they were alone. "Albert," he said, shaking his head, "for Christ's sake, why did you

Charles Pick, father of Albert Pick, Sr., in 1927 at the age of eighty-three.

Albert Pick, Sr.

Gertrude Frank Pick with her daughter Pauline, three years old, and son Albert Pick, Jr., a year and a half, in 1897.

Laurence Pick in 1901   Albert Pick, Jr., then known
by the name Isidore, in 1901.

Dorothy Pick and Pauline Pick Lynne, 1920

Albert Pick, Jr., as a senior
at the University of Chicago,
1916.

Albert Pick, Jr., 1918

Laurence Pick, 1922

Corinne Frada Pick, 1926

have to open your mouth? Now we're both in trouble." Still, the "trouble" was solved, and solved pleasantly: Albert was confined to the military barracks attached to battalion headquarters; no one else was staying there at the time, so he had all the blankets he needed for sleeping, all the books and magazines he could desire for reading; his meals sent in to him, which meant avoiding a cold walk to the mess hall three times a day; and in the evenings, he became a member of the major's regular poker game. It was a punishment he never forgot.

Thereafter, when McFarland wanted Albert to sit in on poker games, he called him to battalion headquarters. The other men in Albert's company would commiserate—"You're in trouble again?"—and off he would go for "special duty that was part of his punishment."

There was a lighthearted quality about all of it that, together with the feeling of comradeship between Albert and McFarland, cast a glow over those weeks in camp. It was all the more memorable for what broke it off. The world-wide epidemic of Spanish influenza reached Camp Grant.

First, one or two men became ill with fever, headache, chills, shortness of breath, aching joints. Then, as if they heralded a wave of the disease, it seemed to strike everywhere at once. One after another reported to his respective sergeant; one after another had his temperature taken and, when shown to have fever, was sent to the infirmary, from which most of them never returned, "except," as Camp Grant soldiers recalled later, "in a box."

In the camp, it was as if war had come earlier than expected. The men felt embattled: they feared the air they breathed, the companions who came too close, the infirmary that seemed a death trap. Albert felt stifled, both by the atmosphere and by the fact that he had been in the camp too long without a break. He asked for, and was granted, a weekend leave. And twenty-four hours before he was due to leave, he began running a fever.

Terrified of the infirmary, he faked health, taking part in full day's march and drill, eating what little he could without throwing it all up, and going through the motions of cleaning his bunk. The next day, he left for Chicago, where he fell at the feet of his mother and sisters and wife.

They nursed him, under the doctor's directions, though there was really nothing much anyone could do but watch the fever rise—Albert's went to 105°—and wait it out. This they did, taking turns by his bed, calming him in his delirium, and calming each other when he could not recognize them or respond to their questions. When his two-day leave was up, Albert, Sr., called Camp Grant and told the battalion commander that it would be some time before Albert could return. He did not add, though the fear filled the house, that he might never return.

The Spanish influenza epidemic of 1917–18 took 20 million lives. No medication was effective; it was virulent in its contagion and its ravages of the body. Albert thought of his recovery as a miracle, and those who loved him agreed. After two weeks, his fever suddenly dropped; and after a few more weeks at home, he was able to return to camp on reduced activity. No one ever knew why some were spared and others succumbed; they sighed and took up the business of living. But for Albert, the experience was added proof—as if the delicate balance of his brother Laurence's health were not enough—of the fragile nature of life and the supreme importance of close human relationships. In a sense, he dedicated himself to both—when he had wealth and could use it to help others to appreciate life and create close relationships.

It was when Albert was transferred from Camp Grant to Camp Merritt, New Jersey, that he was reminded again of the difference in his position from many of his fellow soldiers. The incident began simply, innocuously. Albert asked for early leave one afternoon to spend the evening with friends in New

York, and the request was granted. But, when he went to pick up the pass which gave him until the last ferry boat left New York at 1:00 A.M., the sergeant looked him over—from his slicked-down hair to his smart uniform bought at Marshall Field and Company, to the wrap-around puttees so different from regular army issue, to the sleek shoes made on his own last by his own shoemaker—and barked, "Who the hell do you think you are? An army officer?" Albert said he knew perfectly well who he was; because of shortages in Chicago, those who could, bought their own uniforms; they were encouraged to do so. And now he was leaving to spend the evening in New York, and where was his pass?

The sergeant looked at him. "Well, soldier," he said, "your leave is cancelled." When Albert, caught between surprise and anger, asked the reason, the sergeant told him it was for impersonating an officer.

Arguing did no good; recalling times when he had worn his fine uniform at Camp Grant with the approval of his superiors did no good. His leave was canceled, and he was not allowed to use the telephone to call his friends, nor would the sergeant make the call for him.

There could be a number of reasons for the sergeant's hostility (Albert usually inspired friendship and a genuine liking, so the reaction not only did not suit the occasion; it did not suit the person against whom it was directed) but the most probable was Albert himself. He bore himself with confidence and a self-assuredness found in few of the young men called up to fight the Great War. (Later, when a request came from army headquarters in New York for six men with college educations to work in the army deportation hospital, out of 300 soldiers present, only two, Albert one of them, stepped forward as college graduates. Four others were found who had one or two years of college.) His experience in college and in his father's business had given him a maturity far beyond his years—and the years of many of those who ranked above him. There was bound to be some resentment, especially when he dressed in a manner that set him far apart from the average draftee.

Albert compounded his "offense" with the sergeant who canceled his leave by responding with anger and aggressivity, rather than with the meekness expected of recruits. When the argument reached an impasse, with Albert forbidden use of the telephone and the sergeant reduced to telling him he was in the army and couldn't have things the way he wanted, Albert once more raised the issues of fair play and justice, then gave it up and called the sergeant a son of a bitch, and then, just to make sure the message got through, a bastard.

The reaction was swift. The sergeant told him he was on court martial, and the trial would be held as soon as possible— to which Albert replied that he welcomed a trial, that that was why he had added "bastard" to his first appellation, so there would be no doubt, and that he still had enough faith in human nature to think that few men would condone the arbitrary behavior the sergeant had exhibited that afternoon.

In the words, and in the tone of voice, one could hear Albert giving speeches at the University of Chicago that bored into the professor who had given him a failing grade the previous semester. The sense of outrage at what he saw as injustice, the lack of awe in the face of authority, the steely determination to bring things to a head, the confidence in his own cause—these Professor Nelson had seen, and now a sergeant in the United States army (and later Albert's father). In fact, these were qualities that would characterize Albert Pick, Jr., in business dealings throughout his life, and in his philanthropies as well. They were among the reasons he was widely admired, and—in addition to an old-world charm and quick wit that he developed as he moved more and more on his own into various segments of society—the reasons he was warmly liked; he was seen by most who knew him as a man of swift, honest reactions and a sense of what was "fair" which he carried into all his relationships, however impersonal, however brief.

In the army, however, those qualities could have landed him in deep trouble. In fact, they did not. For whatever motives lay behind the sergeant's arbitrary blockade of Albert's New York evening, the matter never came to a court martial. Albert, pushing his luck, but also rankling with anger, tried to see the lieutenant to force a trial; but the sergeant stopped him, and the matter faded—until a short time later, when the sergeant apologized, chalking the whole affair up to a bad temper and promising to do Albert a favor when he could.

And he did, wangling an assignment for Albert that gave him two days in Chicago with Corinne, followed by another two nights and a day a week later. But even more significant to Albert, because of the added insight it gave him into the people with whom he dealt, was the sergeant's request to *him:* that he help the sergeant write an autobiographical essay required of all those who were applying for commission as an officer. The sergeant confessed to an inability to write well (the essay had to be handwritten) and to spell; he had had very little formal education.

Albert not only wrote the essay from the sergeant's outline, he gave him exercises to improve his handwriting. By the time the sergeant copied the essay, he had struggled for grueling hours under Albert's direction, and his handwriting had improved so that his copy was legible and, indeed, of "passing" quality; the sergeant was soon a first lieutenant.

It was perhaps a small thing, but it was Albert's own; he had devised and implemented a way to help another whose weaknesses were in areas where he was strong. He never forgot the incident, even though it would be greatly overshadowed by the devising and implementation of far larger schemes.

The other major event that influenced Albert's attitude toward military service was a change in his status that allowed

Corinne to join him. He was assigned to the army deportation hospital in Hoboken, New Jersey (as a result of being one of those with college educations), a position which carried with it for married men an allowance for room and board. The army also found a job for Corinne as a file clerk in the Storage Department in New York City at 45 Broadway, in the Battery, at a salary of $1,000 a year. Within a few days of Albert's writing her the news, Corinne was in New York, and the two of them were apartment hunting.

New York was a boom town during the war; apartments were few, and those that became available were snapped up almost immediately. They finally found two rooms in the basement of a doctor's house at 72nd and Columbus Avenue. Two elevated trains clattered overhead, and a subway rumbled below. The neighborhood was dingy, and the trip to work, for both of them, was long. But it was their first home, and they settled into it with the delight of newlyweds finally able to discover each other in private.

It was a good time to be in New York, especially if money was not a problem. Though the army provided barely enough to live on, Albert had his own money; and he and Corinne set out to explore the city with the enthusiasm and curiosity with which they would someday explore far corners of the world. With fifty or sixty theaters from which to choose, they went to a play every weekend and once or twice during the week. They went to the opera frequently, and to recitals; they took excursion trips to neighboring communities and to the major attractions of the city—the Statue of Liberty, Ellis Island, the Battery where Corinne worked, art galleries, museums, and the streets of the city itself, walking and looking and absorbing the sights and sounds of a bustling, prosperous New York.

In the evenings when they did not have tickets for a play or the opera or a recital, they ate at different restaurants up and down the island or at the homes of their friends, especially the Harry Barths—the same ones who had arranged the evening for Albert which had been cut short by a sergeant's bad mood.

It was a good time for both Albert and Corinne to begin their married life as a couple: both were working in useful jobs; they were among millions of strangers and could turn to each other for companionship without the tugs, however loving, of family; and the war cast a spell over familiar things so that they could find in each other their own sense of reality and identity. The bonds they formed in their time in New York would last a lifetime.

So close were they that, when word came one day, following hectic hours of rumors and wild guesses, that Germany had surrendered, Albert called Corinne and told her he had to be with her on this day, at this time, and she was to come to Broad and Wall Street to meet him. He had no idea what he would find beyond his own office. New York City had gone wild; the farther downtown he drove, the denser were the crowds of people and the higher the pitch of excitement. Ticker tape was streaming from windows of brokerage houses on Broad and lower Wall streets; and when that was used up, those who crowded the windows threw torn newspapers and ripped-up telephone books. Albert waded through knee-deep paper, his ears ringing with the sirens that wailed and the bells that tolled, echoing and bouncing off each other as he moved farther downtown. His own blood throbbed with the excitement he felt churning inside him and saw reflected in the faces bobbing close to him. On all sides, he was crushed and kissed and simply touched, as if to touch a man in uniform that day was somehow to participate in the glory that was the end of the war.

In the crowd at Broad and Wall streets, Albert searched for Corinne until he found her and they fought their way uptown to their own special celebration: dinner at the Plaza. They were both in uniform—not the prescribed dress for the Plaza—but on such a day, Albert thought it would not matter.

It did, though not in the way he expected. An anonymous celebrant—five feet tall, white haired and white whiskered (the resemblance to Santa Claus was much discussed), with a large voice—commanded attention in the crowded dining room and offered everyone in uniform any meal on the menu, plus a bottle of champagne, at his expense. They never found out who he was, but Albert and Corinne spent two luxurious gustatory hours, finished the champagne, and then, through streets still crowded, though not as boisterous as earlier, wound their way back to the basement apartment on 72nd street, and, as Albert later recalled, climaxed the day by celebrating "in proper fashion."

And after a two-month mustering out period, and a brief vacation, the young couple returned to Chicago to set up a permanent home and rejoin the business world of Albert Pick and Company.

6

The World of Business

AMERICA entered a new age in 1920—a postwar time of excess and abandon on the one hand, and careful building on the other. It was a time of spending and saving, of inventions, immigration, a changing political scene, shifting moral standards, and movement from the country to the city, that would change the profile of the nation.

Automobiles, railroads, and steamships altered the look and the habits of Americans. They helped create an atmosphere of optimism and expansion; businessmen were looking outward; the idea of movement, if not perpetual movement (but there were some who asked why not), stirred in everyone, even workers low on the economic ladder. After all, if the age was one of expansion outward, why not upward as well?

Growth was the key word after World War I: such companies as the Great Atlantic and Pacific Tea Company bought out over 15,000 small groceries (through 1932); the name "Woolworth" became known in towns from one end of the country to the other (even though most of them called it "the five and dime"); "Piggly Wiggly" and "Stop and Shop" added up to tens of thousands of supermarkets in the first half of the century. Samuel Insull had formed the Commonwealth Edison

Company with an investment of 200 million dollars; he over-saw Chicago's elevated and surface car lines but, leaving something for others, watched while a handful of powerful men stretched the capacities of every part of the city—then becoming known as "the great central market." Figures told the story: 19 million trainloads of animals slaughtered in the stockyards in one year; trading in 69 million bushels of wheat and 99 million bushels of corn; a quarter of a billion pounds of cheese and half a billion pounds of butter shipped into the city from surrounding farms and consumed or packed in half a million cubic feet of cold-storage space or shipped out in refrigerated cars.

Even chewing gum racked up great sales: nearly 30 million dollars worth in the first few years of the '20s—some of which went to build the shining Wrigley Building on the edge of the Chicago River.

Furniture, musical instruments, patent medicines, perfume and cosmetics, cathedral chimes, printing (500 national journals were printed on Chicago presses), electrical appliances, clothing, even coffins—Chicago was the hub, the center, as it had been from the beginning, from before the fire, from the early days when travelers brought back glowing reports of the restless, exciting giant on the shore of Lake Michigan.

And part of that restless giant, making use of it, and reaching into all its corners, was Albert Pick and Company, recovering lost momentum.

It had been a difficult time for many businesses. It was especially difficult for those most vulnerable to wartime restrictions and the advent of prohibition. After passage of the Volstead Act, the Pick supply company, known at one time as the "Saloon Supply House of the World," was left with a huge inventory of bar glassware, liquor bottles and flasks, labels, bottle caps, corks, and bar supplies and novelties. Where it could, it improvised. Whiskey glasses were sold as toothpick holders;

bottle caps and some novelties were shifted to other customers. But in the main, most of the inventory was lost.

What was not lost was the ingenuity of the three men who ran the company at the end of the war: Albert Pick, Sr., his younger brother Hugo Pick and his brother-in-law David Frank, men who saw business as a worthy endeavor for a man's life and who found in solving its problems the satisfactions of creative artists. Prohibition, while a blow, was not a final one: with cajoling, suggestions, and help in planning, the company made it possible for a number of saloon-keepers to convert their establishments to soda fountains, to restaurants, to coffee shops.

The age was especially ripe for soda fountains: they had an aura of the everyday about them that mingled with a romantic air of anticipation. For young people and their parents alike, the soda fountain became a meeting place for day and evening; it even began to figure in novels and stage plays of the time.

All this took new equipment, which Albert Pick and Company had in stock. It took expertise, which the company's staff had in abundance. And it took courage, which the shopkeepers of America drew upon in the years after the war to build Chicago up in their small ways as the magnates built it up in large ones.

In all ways, it was a time of change; and Albert Pick, son and nephew of the men who had come to Chicago to make their fortune in the brash years after the Civil War, knew how to take advantage of postwar years, with their atmosphere of daring, experimentation, and reaching out into areas they might not have thought of had the war not dislocated their lives, their city, and their plans for the future. Albert Pick and his cousins turned their backs on the saloon business as soon as they saw it sliding away in the avalanche of the 18th amendment. They became outfitters of restaurants and hotels; they became part of one of the largest businesses in the country; they became a powerful force in that business and in the mercantile history of Chicago.

It was a story repeated by many far-seeing businessmen in those volatile days when America became a business and industrial force that would dominate world markets for generations to come. Pick was one of those who could see possibilities where others could not, and one who plunged into what others would call a gamble and he would call—with the glint in his eye that often became hard anger or sarcasm but at other times was humor (and not everyone could always tell the difference)—a clear and, in its way, simple, challenge.

He already had expanded, first putting up the new building on 35th Street, then, in 1919, expanding it to more than 520,000 square feet. Then he began insuring a steady supply of goods and services, by buying, or buying into, a number of manufacturing companies. Within a few years, the company was independent in its ability to call on supplies of china (major lines had come from Germany and disappeared during World War I), glassware (they designed their own, sold it to Libby Glass Company, then, when Libby could not deliver fast enough to meet Pick's sales needs, they designed and manufactured another and this time held on to it), silver flatware and hollowware, safety matches, kitchen utensils, linens (designed, sewn, and embroidered at the 35th Street location), floor coverings (Pick and Company became the sole distributors of "Ozite" padding), lunch counters and booths (they made their own at their plant on Wilmot Avenue in Chicago), soda fountains, and billiard and bowling equipment.

From garbage cans to cuspidors, from waffle irons to electric cigar lighters, from barber chairs to whisk brooms to automobile accessories, the company's catalogue grew larger and more elaborate each year, with bold headlines and pages in color to brighten the black-and-white text and illustrations. Catalogues and the goods they displayed were sold to hotels around the country; the business prospered, and the name Albert Pick became a known and honored one, as much for the merchandising flair it symbolized as for the financial success it spelled.

This was the business and the commercial world waiting for Albert, Jr., when he returned from the army at the end of World War I. He knew the company; he had worked weekends and some summer months with a fierce dedication to learning without privilege. He had made it a kind of code, to master his father's business as if he were not his father's son and, to the extent that part-time hours allowed, he had done so. He worked alongside others with diffidence and generally was liked by them, though he was helped by the widespread knowledge that Albert Pick, Sr., seldom seen by any but the sales and executive staffs, but a forceful presence in the showrooms and offices, was the heart of the company and his son was a long way from the seat of power. It is easier to like an heir when he is just at the beginning of his career.

Whatever Albert, Jr., anticipated when he came home from the army, he was not given a place even on the periphery of that seat of power his father and uncles occupied. His father and David Frank and Hugo Pick, with a few trusted long-time associates, ran a tightly controlled and efficient operation; during that time of expansion, swift decisions were made and only later passed on to the workers, Albert, Jr., among them, even when the decision involved selling a subsidiary or branch of the company, thus shutting down an operation in which men and women often had invested thousands of hours and an intense devotion that Albert Pick, Sr., was able to instill. The devotion remained even after he had shut a door in their faces, though many complained that they should have been consulted, to try to "save" their subsidiary or branch.

Albert, Jr., watched it all: his father's enormous energy, merchandising brilliance and steel decisions that strengthened the financial basis of the company. In time, he would match the dedication and doggedness of his father, though in other respects he would soften some of the edges of his father's legacy —perhaps in memory of the wrenching adjustments he had seen the staff of Albert Pick and Company make over the years.

He and Corinne moved into a small house on Cherry Street in the Chicago suburb of Winnetka, and he began work at his father's company in the offices at Randolph and Wells. He was assigned to the office of Adjustments and Complaints—as difficult and thankless a post as could be given him. If he was disappointed, he said nothing. Apparently, it did not occur to him to join another company or to find a place for himself in another field. Since Laurence had gone to Burley's and showed no interest in the business side of their father's company, and since the two girls, Dorothy and Pauline, were not thought of in terms of carrying on the business, Albert was the one to do it, and he took that responsibility seriously. In addition, he liked work, and he liked the work of his father's company. He had been of it, yet apart from it, in his liaison work of supplying cantonments for the army, and he found he was a skillful mediator between people, a thoughtful innovator in material use and handling, and a careful manager. More: he found deep satisfaction in doing each job well—as well as could be done whatever the circumstances—and since he already knew the business of Albert Pick and Company, the chances were he would do his job with more success, and thus more of a sense of fulfillment, there than elsewhere.

In any event, there he was, and he stayed there, though the department his father and uncles put him in was a headache for everyone connected with it, requiring endless patience and Albert's own blend of tact and understanding that soothed others who lacked it. Later, it was the word *sweetness* that would crop up again and again when friends and fellow workers spoke of Albert Pick, Jr. It was a quality that went beyond philanthropies and committee chairmanships. He had a concern for others (a legacy, perhaps, from his tenderness toward Laurence and the semi-invalid status of his mother in her later years) that was remembered with warmth and gratitude and called—though the word often seemed odd in a hard-driving businessman—sweetness.

He dealt with problems and situations that often brought out the worst in people: angry customers who felt they had been cheated in an order, a distraught restaurant owner waiting for a delivery that was late, a furious department manager who had found a defect in a piece of merchandise, or another calling to complain about a discourteous employee of Albert Pick and Company.

Albert dealt with them all, slowly, patiently, calmly. He learned and stored for future reference what it was that pleased and displeased people, what they looked for, what would satisfy them. He came to understand the special relationship between customers and the company with which they did business. And his knowledge expanded even more when, having set the Adjustments Department on a course others could handle, he moved to organize the Personnel Department and learned to look at the company from both management and employee point of view.

He was to stay in the Personnel Department until 1927—serious, quiet, gentle, well-liked by others who had had to accept him as the son of the president but came to admire him and even, frequently, to feel they wanted to help him—another quality that would be of great advantage to him in years to come. That is to say, he was learning to create a business atmosphere that had a large element of the personal, with personal qualities: loyalty, friendship, concern, even shared recreation. This last became a part of the company when Albert organized company barbecues at Ravinia Park (including transportation of the entire staff from executives to freight handlers on the North Western Railroad to Ravinia in the far-off suburb of Highland Park) and a company baseball team that vied with teams from Marshall Field, Carson Pirie Scott, and Mandel Brothers. Uncle Hugo Pick was a star on the baseball team, and Albert took great pride in his batting and fielding skills.

In fact there was a strong sense of "family" in everything Albert did as he learned the business. He was a salesman for a short time, not liking the traveling but doing it because he had to know what the company's seventy-five salesmen felt as they went about from state to state, discovering what new hotels were being built and getting there first to line them up as customers for everything from carpets to bowling alleys, from glassware to bedspreads, before competitors arrived on the scene. He worked for a time, too, in setting up displays in the windows of the store at Randolph and Wells, learning what attracts people, what draws the eye, what holds the attention, what convinces a customer to pay out money for an item.

When he was in charge of the credit department, he discovered an employee, a close friend of his, pocketing part of the cash payments that came in from customers. When Albert had the books audited, he found his friend had made off, over the years, with close to $15,000.

Albert was young, but he handled the problem with skill. He called in the general manager, Julius Cahn (whom Albert, Sr., had lured away from Sears so Cahn could install the kind of efficient systems at Albert Pick and Company he had devised at Sears). Cahn and Albert met with the employee and heard a tale that, had Albert been older, might have seemed sadly familiar: a beautiful wife, an insecure husband, stolen funds for gifts and luxuries to "ensure" a happy marriage.

The next day it was a four-way conference, with the wife learning of her husband's defalcation and using the bookkeeping knowledge with which she had earned her living before she was married to read the auditor's report. The discussion was one of Albert's early triumphs, being resolved with the wife (who, it seemed, loved her husband for himself and not the size of the apartment he had rented for her) going back to work as a bookkeeper, the employee himself taking a cut in pay, and the young couple finding a cheaper apartment and selling half their furniture; all of which, in a relatively short time, led to repayment of the stolen money. The employee was not fired —in fact, he became one of the company's staunchest workers —the marriage weathered its crisis, the financial loss was made up, the episode was not recorded, and Albert had taken his place in the company as mediator and solver of problems. It was a crucial part of his growing up.

◊

But even more crucial were the changes occurring in the company, partly reflecting the shifting currents of those late 1920s, and partly the restlessness of Albert Pick, Sr.

He was beginning to think he was in "the wrong end of the business," as he told one of his department managers, I. S. (Sam) Anoff. He was an innovator, curious and daring, even reckless, in the world of business— far more daring, in fact, than his son would be. In the course of his lifetime he would ride a roller coaster of lost and gained fortunes, his head always high, his dapper figure unbending, the glint in his eye undimmed until the end. So, in 1925 and '26, he was becoming bored and frustrated with the company he had built.

It was not that there were no more challenges: the business was in trouble, with a growing number of unpaid accounts and a peculiar air of uncertainty. It was as if, in the midst of what seemed unexampled prosperity, the supply business was presaging change. Those who could see the ominous signs of the late '20s might have explained it to Albert, Sr., and his brother-in-law as they fought to collect on large accounts they had once thought stable and predictable. But besides the difficulties of the business, Albert, Sr., was restless for new horizons— difficulties of a new kind, less stodgy, as he saw it—and perhaps would not have listened to technical explanations of weaknesses in the present ways the business was being run. So he talked of being in the "wrong end of the business." The real money, the real activity, he said, was in the lease, purchase, and management of hotels.

Buildings and real estate always had attracted him and always would. Chicago itself fed the attraction; it was a construction town, taking puffing pride in dollars, square feet, tallest, broadest, widest, newest in buildings and design. In the three years between 1925 and 1928, the value of construction in the city alone came to 1,390 million dollars in tangible property. The Michigan Avenue bridge had been completed, joining the Drake Hotel on the north and the Blackstone on the south. In 1924, the Wrigley Building had been completed by the firm of Graham, Anderson, Probst and White (which had succeeded the Burnham firm), its white brilliance standing in stark contrast to the gothic gray of the Tribune Tower with its flying buttress at the top that looked, as local observers said, like a spider with eight legs dangling down.

Other buildings were newly built and flourishing, casting Chicago's reputation abroad: the Merchandise Mart with four million square feet of office and showroom space, the forty-one-story Mather (now Lincoln) Tower at Wacker and Michigan, Holabird and Root's 333 North Michigan Building with its round eye of a window looking north across the river, the Chicago Daily News building with its terrace reaching to the river bank, and Samuel Insull's Civic Opera House on an entire block along Wacker Drive.

Chicago meant money; it meant good business. Businessmen traveled the eighteen-hour trip from New York to Chicago and back on the 20th Century Limited; it was such a popular and prestigious train that identical trains were scheduled to leave within minutes of each other so no one would be denied a seat. Perhaps the proudest day of those proud years of America's trains was January 7, 1929, when a fleet of seven matched trains left Chicago for New York carrying 822 passengers, all eating off identical china, wiping their mouths with identical napkins, drinking Apollinaris water and liquor mixed with Cantress & Cochrane Imported Dry Ginger Ale in the newest Pullman crystal goblets.

The men who rode the 20th Century included Albert Lasker, the Chicagoan whose name would be associated first with his brilliant Palmolive soap campaign and then with advertising in general; Seymour Wheeler, the ironmaster; Samuel Insull; and Albert Pick, Sr. The trip was as heady as the air they breathed; expansion and prosperity were bywords, and few cautioned against absolute faith in the future.

From 1926 through the 1930s, Albert Pick, Sr., sailed a course as heady as that of the 20th Century, but far stormier, from one venture to another, from one frantic juggling of events to another, from wealth to bankruptcy and back again. Those connected with him—his brother Hugo, his brother-in-law David Frank, his son Albert, Jr.—rode the waves with him, their lives changing as his did. For Albert, Jr., it would be the beginning of a new era.

It began in January, 1926, when, unknown to the employees and many of the executives of Albert Pick and Company, Albert, Sr., began looking for a buyer for the supply company. That same year, however, in what was perhaps a gesture toward an uncertain future (he thought he might stay as president after he sold, but he was not sure), he began the Pick Benevolent Association with a contribution of one dollar for each share he owned in the company, a total of $350,000. Later, management was assumed by Albert, Jr., his attorney Alan Altheimer and Sam Anoff, but it was Albert, Jr. who built it up so that it became a model of such funds for other corporations around the country in the solidity of its investments and the scrupulous care with which it was monitored.

It took Kleiman until November 1927 to find a buyer; when, by June 1926, Albert, Sr., saw no sign of movement, he thought he would expand the company and so make it more desirable. It was also a way of sharing the collection problems. He chose the highly prestigious New York firm of L. Barth and Company; at the same time he acquired the John Van Range Company, whose standardized kitchen equipment the Pick supply company had sold for years.

Harry Barth, president of L. Barth, had a prestige in his supply business on the east coast equal to that of the Picks in the midwest. But the Barths, too, had a large number of delinquent accounts. Whether either owner told the full financial story to the other is not clear. The merger, in any event, was approved; and in October 1926, Albert Pick-Barth Company was born.

It did not live long.

The frantic quality of Albert, Sr.'s activities probably precluded significant success in any of them in those years. Pick-Barth struggled from its inception; but the driving force, Albert, Sr., could give it only partial and then abstracted attention. In August of 1926 he had formed the Randolph Investment Company for the purpose of leasing, buying, and managing hotels. He had put $250,000 of his own money into its formation and raised close to a million more by bringing his brother Hugo and brother-in-law David Frank in for equal amounts and then by turning to the "family"—the employees of Albert Pick and Company—and selling them shares, up to $10,000 apiece, to be paid for "as they could, over as long a period as they needed."

Most of them bought, though few could reach the limit. The admiration for Albert, Sr., distant and impersonal as he was, pervaded the company. But the Randolph Investment Company enriched no one. The employees received no dividends and, in fact, saw no "return" on their money until late in 1942 when Albert, Sr., began buying back shares from those who wanted to sell. He bought them back over a period of ten years, paying no interest and no dividends.

Oddly, those who tell the story show no resentment. If anything, they recall Albert, Sr.'s business affairs with the admiration for authority's "sharp dealings" that often stuns and frustrates reformers. There were many over the years who did not like Albert Pick, Sr., especially those who had been beaten by him in business or felt the lash of his tongue, but few did not shake their heads in amazement at his willingness to take great leaps, even falls, in the financial world and then bounce back. David Levinson, of the prestigious Chicago law firm of Sonnenschein Berkson Lautman Levinson & Morse, wrote to Albert, Jr., in December 1942, after the Pick Hotels Corporation had gained new vitality,

> I think your father has performed almost a miracle. You, of course, were young and flexible and a 'comeback' such as was made was not entirely unexpected, but for a man of your father's age to retain his enthusiasm, courage and ability to meet new situations is remarkable by any standard that one might use.

But in 1926 and 1927, the Randolph Investment Company was not commanding admiration; it got off to an abysmal start. Its first purchase was the Tuller Hotel in Detroit for $135,000 down. Unknown (though it could have been learned through investigation) was that the hotel had been owned by and was deeply involved with organized crime in Detroit. Within a few months of its purchase, the hotel was the scene of a gangland shooting which destroyed what little potential it might have claimed as a source of revenue for an outside purchaser. Randolph Investment lost the hotel and the down payment.

For novices in the field of hotel buying, it may not have been an extraordinary mistake, but it came at a particularly bad time. During the past several years, Albert, Sr., had been buying land under the umbrella of his Blue Bay Land Company; by 1927 he owned extensive real estate in Florida, Chicago, and the counties and towns neighboring Chicago—Shaumburg, Wheaton, Villa Park, Highland Park. He had invested heavily and steadily; and, when he turned around to dig his way out, he found there were no buyers for the land. The building boom in Chicago was underway, but those who were building had bought their land earlier, at drastically lower prices; no one yet was building in the suburbs or even saw their potential as Albert, Sr., had.

To raise money, he sold his share of Pick-Barth through Arthur Kleiman, who then sold what was left to the Manufacturers' Trust Company of New York. Manufacturers floated a bond of eleven million dollars to purchase and maintain the company in New York and Chicago; the first payments were due in June 1931. The Picks were out; the Barths were out; no one was left at the top who knew the supply business well enough to weather a shift in ownership at any time, particularly the years from 1928 to 1931. Manufacturers offered the presidency to Albert, Jr., at a salary of $75,000 and a New York apartment. Albert was flattered, but he felt his future was in Chicago, and turned down the offer. Manufacturers could not carry the company without him; there was no money to make even the first payment, and the company went out of existence, save for a small Chicago branch headed by former department manager Sam Anoff who, as Albert, Sr., said in a brief moment of sentiment (though whether he thought back to his father and uncle is not known), "kept the name alive."

But he barely had time for sentiment; he was too busy juggling financial crises. For a while, he thought he might make it alone, aloof, faintly amused by others or contemptuous or, to a select few, astonishingly warm. But tragedy was thrusting his family into shock, and the clouds of 1929 were too much for him. For the first time, he brought his son to his side as a confidant and partner.

7

The Family

THE family was a mass of contradictions and strong emotions: in some crucial ways self-sufficient (at least self-absorbed), in others self-destructive, almost always elitist, yet within its boundaries supportive and showing much affection. Of them all, only Albert, Jr., broke away to form a separate life free from Albert, Sr.; and it took many years and personal and national crises to achieve it.

There are men like Albert, Sr., most of them in business or industry, who use the hard-driving world of commerce either to vent or to justify the anger within them. Albert Pick, Sr., channeled his anger into aggressiveness, into taking financial flyers and formulating complicated maneuvers that involved, directly or peripherally, those dependent upon him. The sources of his anger were never made clear; it is probable that they lay in the mixed emotions with which he viewed his music-loving, gambling father, Charles, and his iron-willed mother who kept business and home intact through brutally long days and nights of hard work. His son, Albert, Jr., would be more tolerant of Charles than Albert, Sr., was, though Albert, Sr., supported his father until he died. (He had helped him and his uncle, the first Albert Pick, buy an antique shop after he forced them out of Albert Pick and Company; it was called, many years later, "really a junk shop" and did not last long.)

Whatever the source of his anger, and whatever the forms it took in the world of business and finance, the significant fact of Albert Pick, Sr., was that the anger was often muted in his family life. Though he was capable of roaring or icy tantrums, he could be jovial, affectionate, and helpful to those close to him. He showed concern for their well-being; and he stood ready to offer comfort, if not always help. To the women of the family, he added visible signs of love; to the men (Albert, Jr., Laurence, their cousins and uncles), he was polite and at times showed fondness.

In different ways, both boys failed him, though with Albert, Jr., it was a subtle thing. Laurence, favoring art over business, looking to the Art Institute School of Design rather than a job in the warehouse or office of Albert Pick and Company, was a distinct disappointment. Albert, Sr., thought of him as a sissy, and was never satisfied with anything he did, even taking into account Laurence's childhood bout with rheumatic fever, which had restricted his activities all through school. Still, when it was clear the boy would not go into the business, (in fact, though Albert, Sr., did not know it, Laurence had often begged Albert, Jr., to join him in the ownership of a boutique for women's clothes designed and made by Laurence, the business end managed by Albert, Jr.), finally Albert, Sr., put him into the newly acquired Burley's store.

It was not the paradise Laurence had hoped for, but he knew it was probably the best he could get, and he made the most of it. To handle fine objects, to display them, to talk about them, describe them, watch others' eyes light up when seeing them in a context he had devised, all gave him very real pleasure, and he made that his life.

He was a handsome young man, with a slender face and figure, eyes brown and steady, like Albert's, his mouth softer than his brother's. The two often had their pictures taken together, sometimes dressed as dandies in straw hats and striped blazers; they looked much alike and took pleasure in that. Their closeness had never wavered from the nights spent in whispering darkness before falling asleep in the comfort of each other's company.

In fact, Albert was probably more at ease with Laurence than with anyone else in the family, with the possible exception of his mother. Gertrude was, as her daughter-in-law Corinne said many years after her death, "an elegant woman, a true lady." From the delicate script of her calling card to the even-more-delicate handwriting with which she wrote notes on the back to accompany gifts or to be left at homes where she called, she was a carefully controlled, finely wrought woman who could conceal pain and unhappiness while exacting payment from those around her in the name of love.

In later years, she grew heavy, her face becoming very full; but her smile was extraordinarily sweet, and her features pretty, rather than beautiful or handsome. She was not sturdy (at least, her health seemed fragile and uncertain after two strokes when she was in her sixties plus having high blood pressure most of her life) and she was tended almost as an invalid.

On April 11, 1923, daughter Pauline wrote to Albert Pick, Sr.:

> Mama, I am happy to say, is getting stronger daily, sewing a little, listening to a little reading, and motoring and sitting on the beach [at their winter home in Miami]. She sleeps pretty well and I have given her daily hot baths in the tub which she seems to enjoy. We are taking the best of care of her, suiting our every thought and action to her desires.

She had borne four children in twelve years, had nursed them through the usual childhood illnesses and Laurence's wracking bout with rheumatic fever, learned to keep the house on an even keel during her husband's rages and cold silences, and maintained always a calm and serenity that impressed those who spoke about her, decades later. Whether the strokes actually threatened her life, or weakened her so that invalidism was the only hope for longevity, is unclear. Whatever the outward signs of weakness—easy fatigue and dangerous reactions to stress—she bore three deaths within a decade as she had borne four births and was often the staff upon which others leaned at those bitter times.

It is clear that Gertrude used her family when it suited her; but she did so with humor and affection, so there seems never to have been any resentment. Indeed, there seems never to have been any feeling other than a profound love and determination to keep her well, happy, and cossetted.

"Mama is in bed making lunch," wrote Albert, Sr. whimsically from Miami Beach, "by shelling peas. Soon I will go out to buy lamb chops . . ."

But at the same time, he wrote (in 1932):

> Late this afternoon we are attending the 50th wedding celebration of the Rosens, old time friends of ours, and this evening the Heller Jrs. are playing contract [bridge] with us. Tomorrow afternoon we are going to the races. . . . The balance of the week is too filled with engagements to tell about in my limited time.

Invalidism had its limits.

Gertrude once confided to Albert, Jr., that "no one would ever know" what she went through with his father, but that she "would never complain." There is no question that Albert, Sr., was difficult, demanding, even consuming. Albert, Jr., recalled the time his father was challenged on a point at the dinner table, slammed down his napkin shouting, "I will not take this any more!" and ran from the house, down the broad lawn, to jump into the river at the foot of the property. Whether he did it to cool himself off or to give the impression to his family of a suicidal desperation, he soon came back, remained closeted in his room three days, and "he'd ruined his Patek Philippe watch," recalled Albert, Jr., some fifty years later.

That comment, waspish and still angry, decades later still reflected the anger and terror of the four children who used to run and hide when their father was building to a tantrum. Gertrude could not hide; she sat still, letting the waves of anger wash over her until they subsided in that steely silence (the dash to the river was an exception) which preceded by a day or two a gift of jewelry or flowers to smooth over all the rough spots. Yet that was never enough to make her forget, and often it was not sufficient even to smooth the edges.

Once, he accused her of flirting "like a whore" with a European with whom he had been conducting business the day before they sailed for home. On the boat, he stormed and railed; she did not respond, but tightened her lips and looked past him until he flung himself from their stateroom and paced the ship for hours. The entire journey home was conducted in silence, but she carried with her to her death the sense of helpless fury he aroused in her by his ranting accusations.

Her vivacity sometimes defeated him. Withdrawn, aloof, holding anger back only by giving full rein to aggressiveness in his downtown worlds, he could not match or even fully comprehend Gertrude's gaiety and vivacious greeting of each new day. She played the piano, sang, made up stories for the children and radiated love—even (perhaps especially) at those times when she was using her family to give her a life of royal ease. And Albert, Sr., for all his difficult ways, was bewildered by her, in love with her as much as he could be in love with anyone, and willing to endure the restrictions imposed by her hospital-like regime that was keeping her alive and happy. Gertrude, too, in spite of all she said she had to endure, wrote loving, adoring letters to him when she was in Miami for the winter months and he in Chicago (until he moved to Miami to be with her in 1931). She wrote to him as a woman not grimly enduring her lot but content with her choice. She wrote to him as a woman whose advice was asked about many business matters and who, when it was not asked or when information was not forthcoming, asked to be included in all his dealings, good and bad.

She wrote in an undated letter from Miami Beach (probably in the early '30s, when he was traveling throughout the Midwest on hotel acquisitions):

> My Darling Husband,
> The transaction, with Mr. Eppley, inasmuch as there was no actual expenditure in the transaction, seems a very good one— It is always a pleasure to me whenever you realize on your holdings—there is no use in piling up and cramping yourself to carry a big load.
> What we want to accomplish is to get our affairs so arranged that we can open the Little Home we have planned and start on it as soon as we can organize—I would love to get to work on it as soon as we return—it will make us feel as tho we were doing something constructive and worthwhile . . . dearest, adjust your affairs so that we can feel our way without any embarrassment.

They had been through much together, Gertrude and Albert, Sr., and whatever burdens she bore from his tantrums and the zigzag course of his fortunes (she disapproved of his financial gambles), her love for him seems to have been unwavering, perhaps, though not completely, because he kept her in comfort even when his finances were at their lowest (money, stocks, bonds, and land were held by Albert, Jr., juggled from one account to another, and transferred between the two men or between Albert, Jr.'s account and his mother's, to keep Albert, Sr., afloat). He kept her a part of his maneuvers, telling her some, though hardly all, of what he was doing and writing detailed letters on his travels.

What they had been through might have destroyed other couples. In the course of eight years, three of their children would die—jarring, shocking deaths that tore the fabric they had woven for so many years. Others wondered how they survived. They themselves sometimes looked back and could not fathom the source of their strength. And Albert, Jr., the sole surviving child of that bustling, noisy family, looked back only to remember and to learn; then he looked ahead, to lead.

◊

There had been a time when every Sunday night was family night, decreed by Albert, Sr. Corinne and Albert often resented the command performances; they were young, making friends in the city and the suburb of Winnetka where they lived, enjoying each other's company as their life settled down after the crowded war years in New York. But Albert, Sr., wanted the family together on Sunday night, and so the family was together, trouping into the living room and dining room of the sprawling white mansion on Sheridan Road with its back lawn sloping down to Lake Michigan. There were seven of them: Albert, Sr., Gertrude, Albert, Jr., Corinne, Laurence, Pauline, and Dorothy. The evenings were long, and these seven saw each other constantly, so entertainments had to be devised to make the hours pass: the pool table became the center of competition; costumes were created and plays were produced on the spot; musicales were held with Corinne at the piano and Laurence singing popular songs in his fine baritone; challenge games and quiz games were held with the whole world as subject matter.

There were enormous tensions in this family—resentments, past grievances nurtured, barely submerged angers. But there was love in varying degrees, some of it passionate. Among the family members, that love formed bonds that excluded some as firmly as they tied others together: the bond between Gertrude and Albert, Sr., which opened only to admit fully the two daughters, Pauline and Dorothy; the love between Albert, Jr., and Laurence, born both in Laurence's early illness and poor health and also the sense in both of them that they were not included in the magic circle with their sisters; the strong love between Albert, Jr., and his wife Corinne that had room for all the others as visitors but not participants.

Even that love was tested by the peculiar nature of the family. After they had been married six years, the silent resentment and sense of being unwanted that Corinne had carried within her since the war years burst into the open. She confronted her husband one day with the announcement that she was leaving him.

"I have nothing here," she said to Albert's stunned look. "I have no family, I have no friends, I have no money. I don't even have love. You never tell me you love me, and your family makes me feel that I can never be a part of them. They're like this, your family—" and she made a twisting motion with the knuckles of one fist grinding against the knuckles of the other —"and no one can get inside. I'm not inside, and you don't care, because you don't love me."

Nothing he sputtered and stammered could stop her. She had one confidante in Chicago—a distant cousin of her husband's—who had loaned her train fare back to Seattle, and she had already packed her bags when she told Albert of her plans. Within an hour, she was gone and was on the train for Minneapolis, where she would catch the next train for Seattle.

But on the train platform in Minneapolis, as she was debating where to go for the two-hour layover, she looked up and saw Albert. He had been on the same train, but had not come to her until now; all he wanted, he said, was a chance to talk to her, just a chance to talk. She replied that she had a train to catch for Seattle. "You have at least an hour to give me," he said. He begged. And so they went together to the Nicollet Hotel and sat in a quiet corner of the mezzanine, and Albert got on his knees in front of her and poured out his heart.

It was not easy for him. All his life, he had held back his emotions, not speaking or showing them, as much to keep his father from commenting upon them, disparaging them with his withering sarcasm, as to emulate the unbending man he looked to as model as much as father. Now, desperate, he told Corinne how he loved her, how he needed her, how he looked to the end of each day when he could come home to her from an atmosphere—however much he enjoyed the business aspects of it—that was dominated by his father.

He talked, and she resisted, remembering the family evenings when she was ignored or casually excluded, both Dorothy and Pauline treating her as an intruder into the world they had built around their father and the protection of their mother. But she was in love with Albert, Jr., and he talked until memories of the family dimmed in the sound of his voice and the pleading in his eyes. In the end, they spent the night in the hotel, and the next morning she returned with him to Chicago.

He told her later that he had gone to Pauline when she left, frantic and confused. Pauline reacted immediately. "Go after her; we've never had a divorce in this family." There is no question that Albert loved Corinne and that his love endured as passionately for sixty years. But whether he would have followed her without Pauline's injunction is unknown. He was still in the shadow of his father, and his confusion sprang from early evidence that his father had not approved of Corinne, or of any woman; a wife was necessary to keep Albert out of the army (a ploy which did not work), to protect Gertrude. Corinne was there; Albert seemed taken with her; and so the opposition of her mother was overcome by Albert, Sr., and the rest of them, but not because of any special love for Corinne as the proper wife for Albert. Later, after the war, the family could not even recall exactly why they had encouraged Albert, Jr., to marry at such a young age.

Everything was changed when the two came back from Minneapolis. Pauline and Dorothy, Gertrude and Albert, Sr., greeted Corinne as a reigning princess; they welcomed her with smiles and open arms. (Laurence had liked her from the beginning and had nothing for which to apologize.) The family drew her in and made it clear they wanted her to stay, to be a part of their circle. And they did it well; she felt genuinely liked and cared for (except by Dorothy, where the dislike between them was mutual and just under the surface). Albert, Sr., especially became her friend and, in later years, golfing companion; and Gertrude came to think of her as a daughter, especially when Corinne did such personal, loving acts as making by hand a silver and a gold dress for each of them for their joint wedding anniversaries—Albert, Sr., and Gertrude's fiftieth and Albert, Jr., and Corinne's twenty-fifth —celebrated on December 27, 1942.

So the strands of love and affection twined through the family, not the stuff of alliances (though Laurence often thought of himself and Albert, Jr., allied against the family), but of identity.

The tragedy of Laurence Pick began long before his early death; it began with the rejection by his father of the person Laurence wanted to be. He loved to work with fine fabrics; he loved to handle crystal and glassware; he wrote poems that lacked the originality of true poetry but had thoughtfulness and cried out in every line of loss and aloneness and a clinging to barely-remembered nurturing and love.

Even at Burley's, working in what could have been paradise, Laurence had to prevent himself from dreaming of painting and drawing and the design and execution of magnificent gowns. He was a salesman, and a good one. He was a designer of place settings, and a good one. He enjoyed the designing and tolerated the selling; but even when he had a triumph—an extraordinarily large sale to a customer whose wealthy friends were sure to follow—he could barely interest his father enough to come to the store.

There is no question that Albert, Sr., was disappointed in Laurence, who showed not only no aptitude for the business world, but no admiration, either—who, in fact, barely concealed his contempt for it. (He forgave his beloved Albert for sinking into that world; he accepted Albert's decision as one with no alternatives, given the nature of their father.) But Albert, Sr., was no more disappointed in his son than his son was in him: the cold, remote father who had loaned him money a few times when the growing boy needed it but who could not take the time to come to his son's store to see the displays and hear of the triumphs that would bring Burleys' not only income, but lustre as well.

Gertrude tried to coddle Laurence. After one year at the University High School, she forbade his continuing and had him tutored at home, instead. She and Albert, Sr., took the boy to Europe with them when he was fifteen; she watched over him when he was at home. But she could go only so far; her husband disapproved, and she had to live with him.

How much these tensions worked on Laurence is not clear. Unlike the rest of his family, he was not a letter writer; he confided in no one. Although he had a few friends and a distant relative in Sandwich, Illinois, whom he visited occasionally to get away from his father, essentially he was a loner.

When he died, it was without warning, without a word to anyone that he had not been feeling well. While talking to a customer in an aisle in Burley's in the middle of the day, he dropped to the floor, dead in an instant of a heart attack. He was twenty-five years old.

They had known he was not strong; the early bout with rheumatic fever had left a damaged heart, and he had been warned by Dr. Mercer and then Dr. Black to avoid strenuous activity, stress, and highly emotional incidents. But when he passed his twenty-first brithday with no illnesses, no evident obstacles to a full, normal life, especially in the quiet atmosphere of Burley's, the family had relaxed, had ceased to think of him as different from any of them. Gertrude, it was thought, was the one to cosset, to watch, to fret over. But Gertrude outlived her son and did it with a quiet strength that amazed them, though she withdrew and let her husband write all the letters acknowledging condolences. She also let her husband and daughters take her to Palm Beach after the funeral and wrap her in a cocoon of care that gave them all enough to think about to get through the weeks and months following Laurence's death.

Albert, Jr., stayed in Chicago. He had been home with the flu when Corinne called from Gertrude's house where she had been visiting when the news came. She was crying when she called, and for weeks Albert could not separate in his own mind the tears in her voice, the words she was saying, repeating them when he could not speak, the heaviness of his chest from the flu, and his own tears that stung his eyes and then broke into sobs as he said to himself over and over that his brother was dead.

He had not known much of death; he realized that, of late, he had not known much of Laurence, either. A Laurence who did not need constant watchful protection, who was working in a subsidiary of the company that had little connection with the work Albert was doing, could not be a confidant for a man, grown, married, and struggling to find a niche in his father's company against the entrenched interests of his father's brother, brother-in-law, and long-time workers who were officers of the company.

Now, twenty-seven years old, the only son of his father, he felt suddenly alone. Laurence, not sent for to aid and comfort, but still alive in another corner of their world, had been more vividly a part of him than he had thought. Aside from Corinne, and his mother whom he adored but did not consider a friend and confidante, he felt he had no one on whom he could lean.

He did not think of his sisters in this connection at all. In fact, he thought of them as youngsters (even Pauline, who was older than he by two years) who needed a guiding hand, more gentle and considerate than his father had been with him, but firmer than his father was with them. For it was clear to everyone in the family, aunts and uncles and cousins alike, that Albert, Sr., preferred his daughters to his sons and spoiled Dorothy the most thoroughly.

The two sisters were not close in their childhoods. Pauline, born in 1894, was fourteen years older than Dorothy; and there was little chance that the first-born, and the first girl, would tolerate easily the last-born, and the only other girl. Both were highly intelligent, but Dorothy sparkled, while Pauline was quiet; Dorothy shocked, while Pauline smiled from the sidelines. Pauline probably got a higher approval rating from members of her parents' generation, but Dorothy was well-liked by most of them and by her own generation as well.

Some were to say later that Dorothy lived at the wrong time, that she would have been at home in the 1970s, when women were not frowned upon for living alone, traveling alone, staying out late with young men, and jaunting about the country with them, or with other couples, in their motor cars. She was tall and full-busted, with a long upper lip that she often mocked in letters to members of the family. Bright and quick, she was Albert, Sr.'s "glorious girl," the only one of the family who could, with impunity, speak up to him or answer his intemperate outbursts with intemperate retorts of her own, phrase for phrase. He took delight in her high grades in school, her serious essays, her spirited participation in the Sunday evening family get-togethers, when her costumes would be the most colorful and her charades the broadest of all of them.

Pauline was quieter, more reserved, more conventionally pretty. She wrote poetry, as did her brother Laurence; hers usually ran ten or more verses, often narrative, always rhymed, usually sad or ringing with tones of longing for something gone or something never grasped but glimpsed. She, too, did well in school; and her parents were proud of her. To Gertrude, especially, she was companion, nurse, and friend.

When both girls were older, they drew together. "Isn't it strange," wrote Dorothy to Pauline at a low time in both their lives, "how close we've become in the last few months? After all these years, there are so many things we can talk about. . . ." Their letters, between Chicago and the Broadmoor Hotel in Colorado, where Pauline was staying with her two children while waiting for divorce proceedings to begin from her first husband, were full of personal news, books read (Dorothy "read *Giants in the Earth*—450 pages of fine print—in one day" and loved it; she called it "sort of a *Growth of the Soil*" and recommended it to Pauline for its realism), sights seen, and memories recollected.

Yet the strongest bond was one they never discussed, because they did not recognize it: both girls were dominated by and in a very real way in love with Albert, Sr. They would have been appalled, all three of them, and Gertrude as well (for the girls genuinely loved their mother), to have heard it thus articulated; but it was this passion, running beneath all that they did in the years of their growing up and their maturity, that prevented Dorothy and Pauline from escaping the childhood boundaries of family, just as it was Laurence's fear of his father that kept him selling at Burley's rather than opening a boutique or setting up a studio of his own. The sudden deaths of all three of them in early adulthood could be seen at least in part as an element of the stress of their relationship with their father; the only one of the four children to live to old age and live a full, independent life was Albert, Jr., whose first break with his father came when he followed Corinne to Minneapolis and asserted himself as her husband when they returned to Chicago, and whose even more dramatic break would come very soon, while he was still young.

Pauline married a businessman and dabbler in financial affairs when she was almost twenty-eight. Some said she became fearful that she would never marry and chose Arch Lynne because he was the best of those she could hope for. But there was probably more to it: Lynne (his real name was Levy, but Pauline insisted he change it before they married) was a rough man, his language coarse, his behavior direct, sometimes brutal. No man was more directly the opposite of Albert, Sr. She may have known she was making a match that could

not last, and thus would not affect the strength of her attachment to her father, or she may have been trying to see how far
she could move from his sphere. Whatever her thoughts, and
no one in that family of much talk and constant letter-writing
knew what they were, the marriage was uncomfortable from
the first. When no children came, two were adopted, John and
Gertrude, but the "creation" of a family did not help. Pauline
was wretched, as she finally told her father in 1927, and was
leaving her husband.

"How you kept your misery from us for so long is something
I will never understand," wrote Albert, Sr., to Pauline in
Colorado; in fact, he was as angry for being kept out of her
thoughts as he was sympathetic to her unhappiness. But once
she poured out her grievances and loneliness, the letters from
Albert, Sr., and Albert, Jr., too, were warm, supportive, and
businesslike with the details of the divorce. The two men took
over and led Pauline, as if by the hand, through the steps
to her freedom. "Everything is breaking as we thought it
would. . ." wrote Albert, Jr., of their conversations with Lynne
and the lawyers; and she let them break as her father and
brother directed.

If she felt she would rather have undertaken these procedures herself, as elements of her own independence, she did
not say so. If she ever did think it, the thought passed. "My
dear ones," she wrote while en route to Colorado on the
Capitol Limited on June 23, 1929, just after her divorce had
become final:

> It is nearly two hours since I left you all, and I have just
> remained sitting quietly, and thinking such happy contented
> thoughts. How fortunate I am in having such dear ones who
> reciprocate the love I have for them! After all, everything we
> do, and feel is made joyous by love. It is so easy to love and
> be happy! Believe me to be sincere when I tell you that the
> happiest and finest thing in my life is my love for you.

Through the trials I have experienced you have been my sustaining support. And now that I am facing a new life—have already started on it—there is joy singing in my heart and a great thankfulness.

To you, Mama and Papa, I owe all the fineness of my nature, and too, all the material pleasures which you have given me in abundance. How can words express what I would say?

She had more confidence after the divorce than before she had married Lynne, but it still was not enough to break away from her parents—her father, because of the constant spell he exerted upon her, and her mother, because of the increasing invalidism that kept them all on tiptoe around her. Gertrude had "miraculously" (wrote Pauline from Miami) withstood the shock of Laurence's death—their terror for her survival remained in their memory as the chief emotion they felt after the boy's death and during the months following—but they were convinced another shock would kill her, as would any great excitement or stress, and they dedicated themselves to keeping her world quiet, serene, and entirely predictable.

The combination of a mother balanced on a precipice and a father longed for and adored kept Pauline in a state of tension she herself probably did not recognize. She stayed in Colorado for a time after her divorce, then took a trip to Europe, writing home and being written to daily, where she met a charming, much-traveled American businessman named Charles Staiger and thought her life had changed. "We are so in love," she wrote and later, in a postcard to Dorothy in January, 1931; "We are so happy, my husband and I. . . ."

But Charles Staiger was not aggressive and was not likely to be; he had been successful as a vice-president of Harry Winston's jewelers but had never branched out on his own; in general, he retired from any arena where there was conflict or where he would have had to push his way in to make an impression or even to be a part of a business scheme. Again,

Pauline had chosen a man whose chief characteristics stood in direct opposition to her father's.

What might have happened to the marriage was never known. In March of that year, Pauline became ill in Miami, where she and Staiger were visiting her parents. At first, it was pneumonia, and they were concerned but not alarmed. Pauline, at the time, was a robust woman, who, she said, was truly happy for the first time in her life. But the pneumonia was a forerunner; in 1931, with antibiotics still far in the future, diseases of the lungs often were complicated by empyema, an accumulation of pus in the pleural cavity, the space between the lung and the chest wall. In Pauline, the condition was particularly virulent, and neither surgery nor the insertion of drainage tubes were sufficient to cure it. She was hospitalized through April; and in May, she died. She was thirty-eight years old.

Again, they tried to shield Gertrude. And again, Gertrude was the one to stay firm in the midst of overwhelming shock. Every day through that terrible spring, Albert, Sr., had sat in Pauline's hospital room writing to Albert, Jr., in Chicago detailed reports on her temperature, the "savage wound" in her chest from the surgery and drainage tubes, her pain, and her pleas that he not leave her to return to Chicago. "None of my business in Chicago is as important as Pauline's recovery," he wrote; and he stayed, through some of the most complicated and threatening times of his financial life, which Albert was handling in Chicago. Those daily letters he wrote to his son mingled news of Pauline with orders to shift money from one bank to another, to sell *these* shares but transfer *those* to Gertrude's name, to look at one property while trying to sell another. He sent telegrams, he wrote long, scrawled letters sent special delivery, he wrote memos and notes and single lines on postcards. And all the while, he was listening to Pauline's labored breathing and telling her he would not leave her until she was well.

It seems he did not allow himself to think she would not recover. Of the two doctors attending her, he told Albert, Jr., he believed the more optimistic one, as he seemed to know more about the case. He kept track of Pauline's fever-free days but did not count the ones when her temperature rose to 103 or 104 degrees. He gambled on her health as he gambled in real estate, looking only for promise. As with the hotel in Detroit, he did not look behind the words or beneath the visible facts. Nor did he tell Gertrude all that he wrote to Albert, Jr. Gertrude came to the hospital two or three times a week; and both Pauline, sick as she was, and Albert, Sr., put on cheerful faces and spoke of what they would do when Pauline came home. Gertrude probably knew what was happening; she knew more and could take more than the family thought; but if she did, she did not tell anyone. She allowed them to try to delude her into sureties of the future; but when the future came, with Pauline's death, she was again the strongest and helped the rest of them bear their pain and shock.

For Albert, Jr., and Dorothy, it was a terrible time. Parts of them had died, pieces of the family unit they had counted on as a rock behind and under them for so long. The tensions of the family, the stresses caused by Albert, Sr.'s fierce temper and domination, were forgotten, as domination tottered beneath forces none of them could defeat.

Yet, after Pauline was buried and the men turned again to the financial struggles that were engrossing them, Dorothy found it impossible to stay home. Gertrude had taken Pauline's two adopted children, John and Gertrude (she and Albert, Sr., would soon adopt them), and was finding in them the pleasure she had missed after her own grew too big to need mothering. And Dorothy, perhaps because she felt Gertrude was hapily occupied, perhaps because of her previous traveling, as much to get away from Albert, Sr., as to see the world, began to travel again. She thought of herself as an artist—as had Laurence, she had studied for a time at the Art

Institute of Chicago and had spent two summers at the Berkshire Summer School of Art in Monterey, Massachusetts—but serious painting and drawing did not keep her involved. She made her own Christmas cards—vigorous, lively, pen-and-ink colored drawings of jazzy cars and girls with cloches and long scarves whipped by the wind, wishing her friends "plenty of Christmas cheer" from Dot Pick. She sketched scenes on her travels around the country, to Cuba and Europe, and illustrated letters she wrote home. But none of it had come to anything by her mid-twenties beyond diversion. When she was twenty-four, she begged her father to give her something to do in Albert Pick and Company; he named her Vice-President and gave her the responsibility for decorating the hotels they were beginning to buy under the banner of the Randolph Investment Company.

She had not studied interior decoration, but she tried and was pleased with the lobbies and rooms that bore her stamp. Some said she had no taste, and changed the rooms back as soon as she left; but most found her so charming and lively they overlooked her weaknesses as a decorator and asked her to come back soon.

She charmed most who met her. Men from every country she visited—Amsterdam, Hungary, France, England—wrote to her for years after she had been there. Others, in America, sent her telegrams announcing their impending arrival in Chicago or Miami or Colorado—wherever she was perched at the time. She saved dance programs with pieces of the chiffon from her stoles tucked away inside, next to the loving inscriptions from the men with whom she danced.

There were those who would call Dorothy promiscuous. Whether she was sexually involved with the men she knew is uncertain but it would seem extremely doubtful. In the letters she wrote home while traveling (writing daily, firing off short and long letters usually written late at night before going to sleep so she could give detailed descriptions of the hours she

had just spent and the people with whom she had spent them)
she appears to have been unable to relate with any real warmth
or affection to the men who followed her about. Those feelings
were reserved for her father.

"Couldn't we meet in New York for a day or two?" she
wrote Albert, Sr., in 1931, when she was twenty-four years
old. "We could have a real honeymoon; you're the only one I
want to have one with. . . ."

It was an innocent letter, as it was an innocent, but devastat-
ing, relationship for the young girl who could not find in the
young men who flocked about her an image to eclipse her
father's. And so she traveled and wrote to her parents with an
intensity that filled her days so that their emotionless quality
was masked. Her last trip was to Europe, in 1933, where she
visited friends she had made on earlier trips and rented a car
to motor through southern France. Shortly after she returned,
while staying with her parents in Miami, she began getting
dizzy spells and soon was unable to keep her balance. She
was put to bed but did not improve. A few months later, she
died of what was called a brain tumor, although family members felt the doctors, who were at a loss throughout her illness,
perhaps had misdiagnosed the problem in the first place and
might have saved her, had they known more. She was buried
in April, 1934; she was twenty-eight years old.

The blows had come too fast; this one struck them dumb.
Condolence letters were answered by Albert, Sr., as before.
Gertrude stayed in her room; and Albert, Jr., and Corinne
stayed with her, unable to comprehend what had happened
within the space of a few years.

There was nothing to be done but to pick up the pieces, and
they did it with the family still struggling through darkness.
Albert and Corinne had had a daughter in 1927; and Albert,
Sr., and Gertrude adored her, as they loved the two children
they had now adopted since Pauline's death. They drew themselves to the children as to lamps where they could warm them-

selves. The three became all their children and the children of all the family. But even their glow could not completely chase away the darkness—especially since some of it came from beyond the family: from the economic and social disruptions of America in the mid-1930s. And those problems had to be faced and conquered, whatever happened within the walls of the family.

8

Bankruptcy and Beginnings

THE foresight of Albert, Sr., that led him to purchase what would become some of the most valuable land in America (including the first and second circles of suburbs ringing Chicago and, later, land at Bal Harbor and Bay Harbor in Miami Beach) did not always extend to his choice of times in which to buy. His Blue Bay Realty Company held whole towns (many of the streets in some of these Chicago suburbs are named for members of his family); the Randolph Investment Company was buying hotels in towns from Detroit, Michigan, to Waco, Texas; briefly, there was the Albert Pick Investment Company, but he barely had the stationery printed before he abandoned it for lack of adequate capitalization.

He was everywhere and, in a sense, nowhere. His son was becoming more deeply involved with hotels—buying, managing, making plans, in his steady, careful way—and Albert, Sr., was frustrated and often impatient with the plodding sense of day-to-day business which seemed to him to characterize activities he once had seen as exciting.

There were other problems as well. Relations with Albert, Jr., were difficult. For a short time, the two of them had been, if not close, at least amicable and respectful. Albert, Sr., liked

Corinne (the two would become good friends on the golf course and off it); and Gertrude and Corinne, too, would create a special mother-daughter relationship that gave the family, and especially Albert, Jr., pleasure. But, while the two men, father and son, had shared the grief of Laurence's death and shared as well a concern over Gertrude's frail health, they could not share their business—the foundation of their lives and the support, psychic and financial, of almost every member of their extended family.

Albert, Jr., had been "working his way up" and had not complained about the slow pace or the sense of distance from the top he felt every day of every year. The top in the '20s had meant his father, his two uncles, and a few trusted lieutenants; they did not move over to make room for the next generation. Yet he made no fuss, but went on smoothing the problems of difficult departments to which he was assigned, remote from the centers of decision-making.

There had been one exception. Soon after his twenty-first birthday, he was invited to attend a board meeting of the Albert Pick Supply Company. His father, as Chairman, dispensed rapidly with old business, then declared the meeting open to discussion of filling a vacant place on the Board. David Frank, Albert, Sr.'s brother, nominated Albert, Jr., a vote was speedily taken (it was unanimous), and the young man found himself shaking the congratulatory hands held out to him.

He and his father never discussed it, but he always was sure the idea was Albert, Sr.'s, given to David Frank to initiate in the meeting. He was touched by the evidence of his father's faith in him, and even by the quiet way in which the business was handled. Of course his father might have said something to him, something personal and private; but his father never did, and the moment when he might have done so passed forever.

Yet, surely with his father's approval, he began to gather authority into his hands, however slowly, and in 1927, with the family out of the supply business and venturing into new fields, Albert, Jr., was named Treasurer of the Randolph Investment Company.

With his father and uncles and a few men who would form the solid core of the hotel business, Albert worked in that early time to build a company in which he already felt strong pride and a confident sense of the future. The only clouds—and they would grow rather than diminish—were those shadowing his relationship with his father.

Their first real clash over business came in 1928, when Albert, Sr., invited his son as treasurer of the company to join him in one of his periodic trips to New York to arrange lines of credit with a number of banks. It had been a feature of Albert, Sr.'s success in the supply business that he could furnish a complete hotel for sums ranging upward of half a million dollars and extend time payment privileges to the buyers. No other supply companies had lines of credit that would allow that. (The only serious competition came from Marshall Field and Company, the department store whose roots went back almost as far as the Albert Pick Supply Company.)

The two Alberts, father and son, went to New York in 1928 for the first time as fellow officers of their company. Albert, Jr., was impressed with the seriousness of the occasion. When he was introduced to a vice-president of Morgan Guarantee named Grant Johnson, he marshaled his facts and, as the conversation went on, was able to step in, when his father hesitated, with exact figures on the past year's volume, open account credit, inventory, accounts receivable, and on through the financial affairs of the company. He was absorbed and eloquent, happy in the knowledge and experience he finally was using and in the presence of a New York banker who was clearly pleased at his command of facts and figures.

But his father had gone quiet, very still, his thin lips in a rigid line. When the conversation ended, he ordered his son to write Johnson a letter from Chicago with exact figures on all the categories they had discussed. Johnson shook his head.

"Won't be necessary, Mr. Pick. I'm impressed with your son; he knows what he's doing. The figures are in line with last year's; they show you've made good progress. I don't see any problem with extending the half million credit for another two years. I congratulate you on your new treasurer." He turned to Albert, Jr., and invited him to have lunch "whenever you're in New York."

The quarrel that followed was not their first; but it was one Albert, Jr., never forgot. They stood in the imposing marble lobby, talking in low tones. "This is the last time," his father said, "that I ever take you on a trip with me. You humiliated me. You showed me up most artistically. I felt like two cents. You're not coming with me to any more banks on this trip; I don't need you. I've been handling my own affairs for years, and I can continue in the same way."

Albert stammered that he'd thought his father would be proud of him; but his father, taut with fury, continued to rail, bitterly and very quietly, oblivious to the people and the splendor of their surroundings, for nearly an hour. Albert, Jr., moved from bewilderment to anger. Finally, Albert, Sr., told him to go off with his friends while he did the work he'd come to New York to do. And he left. Albert, newly a treasurer, newly a family man and becoming a man of substance, was left standing in the lobby of the bank, not even the "half an adult" he had felt for some months his father was finally beginning to treat him.

It was a pivotal time. Albert, Sr., had been enormously successful in the supply business, guiding it to a peak volume of 30 million dollars a year. He was wealthy and respected, if not loved. But he had been gambling in land and buildings since 1926, buying in great gulps everything from small one-acre farms to such buildings as the Reliance Building on Chicago's State Street (later named a landmark under the 1970s preservation act) and several square blocks along the Chicago river between Monroe and Madison streets, fifty years later to shine as the Riverside Plaza financial and business district.

He may have been impatient with Albert, Jr.'s slower way of making decisions and expending funds; but, in fact, Albert, Jr., was keeping the Randolph Investment Company alive from day to day while the clouds of 1929 were just appearing on the horizon. The company had made a shaky beginning, but the times were both good and bad for hotel purchases, and Albert, Jr., was learning how to use the times to advantage.

He also, and his father could not forget this, had stayed out of a financial plunge that had badly burned his father: the purchase of stocks from the charismatic Jonas brothers of New York who built an empire on paper and took a number of investors with them when they fell in 1929. In not exercising his option to buy stocks, Albert, Jr., had followed the advice of Henry Russell Platt, lawyer and family friend, who had said he "didn't like the smell of it: like a super colossal confidence game." But Albert, Sr., stayed in and lost heavily. It had been the first time Albert followed Platt's advice rather than his father's lead.

By the time the collapse of 1929 was imminent, Albert, Sr., held a fistful of installment contracts with which he had bought thousands of acres of land on which he could neither build nor keep up payments and for which he could find no buyers, and he had mortgaged some of his holdings in the city of Chicago. In addition, he had used his name and his wife's personally to guarantee bonds which he had borrowed in order to loan money on a piece of property next to the Insull Building (later the Civic Opera Building). The guarantee had saved him one percent on the interest on his own loan; but in 1929, the face value of the bonds went to nothing, and his business became subject to the trusteeship of those who had bought the bonds, thus becoming entitled to receive a percentage of all property sales Albert, Sr., made to the total value of the bonds.

But before the crash, there had been another question of bond guarantees Albert, Sr., was negotiating in order to build in the several-block area he had purchased along the Chicago River. A parcel owned by the estate of Marcus Marx, of the clothing company of Hart, Schaffner and Marx, adjoined his land; and Albert, Sr., wanted a ninety-nine-year lease to build an office building already being designed for him by the architectual firm of Graham, Anderson, Probst and White. The blueprints called for caissons reaching to bedrock level. Lessing Rosenthal, lawyer for the Marx estate, balked, saying if the building was a failure he would be stuck with extraordinarily expensive caissons whose cost he could not recoup from tenants. Albert, Sr.'s investment banker, M. E. Greenebaum, said his client would guarantee the building costs; Rosenthal and the estate would lose nothing.

The dickering dragged on; Rosenthal went to Europe for a vacation, infuriating Albert, Sr., who already had leases from business firms and public utilities for space in the unbuilt building. He needed the income desperately, but first he had to have the building. He called in his brother-in-law David Frank to act as go-between to offer to buy the parcel outright from the Marx estate for one million dollars. Rosenthal, when approached, would refuse to sell; but before that happened, Albert, Sr., took out a mortgage on the other properties he owned in the same area along the river (to have the money ready when Rosenthal returned from Europe) and, as before, personally guaranteed it. But in order to get the interest down a full percentage point, he also promised that his wife and son would join him as guarantors.

Fifty years later, Albert, Jr., recalled that "there was no one in Chicago I revered more than Henry Platt." The lawyer had acted as advisor and something less than father but more than friend for years. He owned the Reliance Building with Albert, Sr., and had prevented him from selling it at an earlier time when Albert, Sr., had been financing another deal. Unable to

sell without Platt's signature, Albert, Sr., said he would mortgage his share and personally guarantee it for the best deal.
Platt raised his voice against the proposal, and Albert, Sr.
raised his. "You'll never make a big fortune," he said, "being
so cautious."

"I have a fortune," Platt answered. "And I'm satisfied with
what I've got. Listen to me: don't ever guarantee a mortgage or
bond issue. I'm glad young Albert is here to hear this," he
added, turning to the younger man. "You can lose everything."
Albert, Jr., never forgot it.

Barely a year later, his father stood in Albert, Jr.'s office at
the Randolph Investment Company with a mortgage for him
to guarantee with his signature. Albert, Jr., hesitated, as he
later recalled, "about 30 seconds," and Albert, Sr., "blew all his
fuses." Albert shouted over his father's shouts, "Dad, I'm over
twenty-one. The mortgages look pretty good, but you shouldn't
have guaranteed them."

Albert, Sr., jumping to the thoughts he knew were in his
son's head, shouted, "You think Platt knows more about real
estate than I do. Mr. Platt is not going to make my deals."

"If your deals incorporate me," Albert, Jr., answered, trying
to hold his voice down, "don't I have a right to think them out
and talk them over with Mr. Platt?"

His father's body became rigid with anger. "You do what
you goddam please."

"I'm young," Albert, Jr., went on, "and I intend to build
more slowly. I don't want—"

But his father was leaving the room, "I'm through," he
shouted over his shoulder, and moved that day into a vacant
office in the suite of the lawyer I. B. Lipson, a long-time friend.
Albert, Jr., called his mother to ask her to stop his father from
guaranteeing the mortgage; but Gertrude told him not to
oppose Albert, Sr. "I'll do anything he wants," she said, "and
you should, too. If he wants you to sign it, then sign it."

"It's a good deal," Albert, Jr., said. "Dad doesn't need to

save that interest." It was the last time they spoke of his signature directly; it was an issue, however, in the break that would occur when his father's house of cards collapsed and he went thorugh bankruptcy a few years later.

۞

In his carly years in the hotel supply business, Albert had spent some months traveling with the company salesmen, listening to their dialogues with customers, poring with them over the catalogues they flourished when describing the latest in bowling equipment or dust pans or monogramed glassware or bed linens. By the time he began to manage various departments in the main office, he knew a number of hotelmen around the country and, from conversations and correspondence with them, had a good knowledge of the problems of hotel management. In fact, long before he himself became what friends affectionately called "one of America's leading innkeepers," he felt he knew more about that complicated business then many of those already engaged in it.

Perhaps it was simply the idea of travel that made hotels interesting to him; whatever it was, he always saw in them something more than the physical structures he would be buying, selling, and managing for most of his business life. They were, first of all, conglomerates of people with whom he would deal on a personal basis with such success that, years after he had sold the Pick Hotels, others would recall that "people worked for Albert rather than the company; they felt loyal to *him,* not to any one hotel or group of hotels."

And as well as being people, hotels also were way stations with all the excitement that implied—far more in the 1920s and 1930s than in the 1970s and 1980s, since air travel has turned far-flung cities into near neighbors and made the business of moving from one point on the map to another as unremarkable as crossing the street to buy a newspaper. Corinne would later reminisce about their travels to Europe on the

Queen Elizabeth and the Mauritania; about steamer trunks and life aboard the leisurely, elegant ocean liners that turned every trip into a romance from its first day. And Albert would remember in detail the honeymoon trip he and Corinne took in Texas, when they were caught in a surprise blizzard as they drove near Waco. During the time they waited for a new engine block to be delivered so they could drive their car—a victim of the cold—back to less primitive surroundings, they had to stay in a tiny hotel with no heat or private bath facilities other than a pitcher of water that had a layer of ice on it each morning. By the time he recaptured the mood of those few days, the hotel had taken on the same glow he and Corinne had on their honeymoon; Albert's feeling of the excitement of hotels was undimmed.

He plunged into the hotel business of the Randolph Investment Company, then, not only with the determination that marked all his business activities, but also with the feeling that this was a field in which he could build and create with interest and enthusiasm.

For all the knowledge Albert had about hotels, he and his uncles and father were aware of their inexperience, and at first, they confined themselves to buying a half-interest in hotels owned by long-time customers who needed extra capital. But Albert, Sr., could not abide the shared decision-making and sense of incomplete ownership; and Albert, Jr., too, though he might have waited a while, agreed that they should buy outright or sell those half-owned hotels. Like his father, he wanted to build a strong business that was fully theirs; having known the solid satisfaction of owning one business that was among the most respected and successful in the country, both Albert and his father could not be satisfied with less than another experience of the same kind.

Besides, he was learning. It was, of course, one thing to sell supplies to customers in established hotels and another to manage those hotels. Albert had suddenly found himself in the midst of a "crash course" in hotel management at the same time as he was struggling with the daily problems of the financial management of individual hotels. The debacle in Detroit, when the underworld held one of its murders in the lobby of the Randolph Investment Company's newest hotel, shook him badly; and he became even more cautious than before. This was the time, in 1926 and 1927, when his father was moving buildings and land as if they were chess pieces on a board of his own devising; he left Albert, Jr., to manage the hotels, though he kept enough interest in them to have a couple that were considered "his." In general, however, Albert, Jr., was clearly, from the beginning, the "money man" in the family hotel business. For all his earlier assumptions that he knew more about managing than the managers, he never excelled in that part of the business. Two strong men did: Edgar Moss and Harold McCormick would become the day-by-day supports of the company, as Albert refined that special financial genius that would allow him to expand operations and his own sphere of activities and retain full control, even as he and Corinne spent winters in Florida and traveled abroad.

It was not only financial genius that kept the new business steady through the errors of the first few years and then through the depression. Two factors were paramount. One was Albert's stubborn doggedness; he would not admit defeat nor allow others to think that he was ever losing confidence. It was that stubbornness that sent him, with Moss and McCormick, to visit their hotels at the worst times of the depression and give instructions to the staff (and show them how to do it) on turning on and off lights in all the rooms at regular intervals until midnight or later to give the impression that the places were booming. It was theatrics, but it was better than allowing dark hulks to sit in the saddened towns of depression America; and it also made possible the continuance of certain lines of credit as word got around that the Pick Hotels seemed busy in spite of everything.

But in the long run, theater could not carry a struggling business. The prices Albert and his father had paid for hotels in 1927 and 1928 had been unrealistically high, reflecting the whole giddy economy of the time. When the collapse came, there was a period when the company could not meet the full payroll, could not pay interest or amortization on mortgages, could not pay purveyors in full. Something always was paid; and Albert made regular visits to banks which had loaned them money, to vendors, to employees, explaining, explaining what everyone knew: there was not enough money to pay all the bills.

They were not sued by any bank, insurance company, or individual. This was Albert's triumph in those years; he kept the company afloat, kept suits and demands at bay (giving up, in the process, superbly advantageous discounts offered in exchange for cash—which he did not have—by suppliers badly in need of money), and maintaincd a spirit of optimism among those who worked in the Chicago office and on the staffs of the hotels they owned. Eventually every debt, meticulously recorded in Albert's books, was paid back with interest.

As the supply business had changed with the passage of the 18th amendment, so the hotel business changed with its repeal in 1933, albeit less drastically. Business slowly improved, some lines of credit were restored or expanded, and Albert was able to buy a number of hotels through insurance companies which had foreclosed on mortgages. He bought many on an earnings basis, others with small downpayments, long amortizations, and low interest rates. Earnings were steadily plowed back into the company; and by 1938, Albert was able to joke with the accountants and lawyers who had recommended voluntary bankruptcy to him in 1931 and 1932.

❦

Bankruptcy already had been a reality in his life. Through long, draw-out years, his father had fought to retain something from an involuntary bankruptcy proceeding filed against him in 1933; Albert was central to the proceedings and to his father's twists and turns.

In 1933, when the petition was filed, Albert, Sr., showed direct and indirect obligations of approximately four million dollars. To raise some immediate cash, more for "breathing space" than anything else, Albert, Jr., conceived and organized the K and A Corporation, capitalized at $100,000, to buy that amount of stock in the Pick Hotels Corporation. The initials stood for Katz and Altheimer—Siegmund Katz, accountant for the Picks, and Alan Altheimer, their attorney—who put up the first money; but the moving force was Albert, Jr., who polled the family, first and second cousins all of whom had been working for Albert, Sr., for years, and asked each of them for $5,000. He collected about $35,000, and the remainder he put up himself. Albert, Sr.'s, stock in the Pick Hotels Corporation and some of his North Shore real estate was sold for $100,000, which went to Albert, Sr.'s creditors.

Albert, Jr., also undertook to sell his father's lavish lakefront home in the Chicago suburb of Winnetka (later to be the home of insurance man Clement Stone); and, on their regular trip to Miami that winter of 1932–33, he and Corinne found and bought a home there for Albert, Sr., and Gertrude. At the same time, in Chicago, the Board of Directors, under Albert's direction, named Albert, Sr., Chairman of the Board and Albert, Jr., president of the Pick Hotels Corporation.

When the sum of the events of these years are totaled, the unbelievable stress put on the family is starkly clear. Pauline died in 1931; and Dorothy, in 1934. The depression struck just as the Randolph Investment Company was being renamed—amid high hopes and plans—the Pick Hotels Corporation, Albert, Sr.'s house of notes and bonds and mortgages was collapsing about him; and Albert, Jr., was struggling with a new company and an old set of tensions with his father.

The relationship between the two men went through a

number of wrenching stages in the 1930s. On the surface they were friendly, cordial, even affectionate. Their letters are perhaps a trifle formal for father and son (Albert, Jr.'s more so than his father's), but they communicated throughout the period following Albert Jr.'s refusal to guarantee his father's bonds and through the period when it was the son who was pulling the father out of bankruptcy. In fact, though, Albert, Sr., never got over the dependence upon his son in that first bankruptcy crisis and its continuation through the resolution of 1937. It rankled for the rest of his life and burst forth at unexpected times, in connection with diverse—but always business-oriented—issues. Some years later, he threatened to sue Albert, Jr., for one million dollars for having cheated him in the transactions of the bankruptcy settlements; but he never went further than talk. It was an outburst of a tired, frustrated and lonely man lashing out after his wife's death for someone, something to blame for his unhappiness.

At the time the K and A Corporation bought his shares for $100,000 and Albert found him a new home in Miami, Albert, Sr., left the Pick Hotels Corporation for the last time. He felt betrayed by the Board which had elected his son president, shunting him to a position with no authority; and he was furious at the prospect of working with (perhaps for?) a son who was managing to salvage something from the catastrophes which had almost swallowed the father whole.

He spent the next four years juggling funds to retain something from the bankruptcy, and dabbling in ventures that glowed, in the beginning, with signs of wealth. The first was the Pick Importing Company, organized in 1933, to buy and sell whiskey. Through the Hotel Antlers in Indianapolis, which the company had owned for a short time, he had met a man named Arthur Baynham, who was looking for whiskey to buy and resell; and in September, he went to London to find the whiskey. Baynham followed in October; during the time he was alone, Albert, Sr., wrote long letters to Gertrude, describing his constant colds ("This city is a terrible place for a foreigner ... the town is damp due to the daily rains ... no heat in the rooms ... it seems everywhere one goes a draft follows him. Accordingly I took cold, my nose is running like a hydrant.") and his business dealings, from the cost of whiskey to its age and quality.

In the end, he sold Baynham 1,000 cases of ten-year-old Scotch whiskey ("There is very little whiskey in the entire United Kingdom of this age and quality," he wrote Gertrude) at a profit of $3,000. He had lined up another set of purchases of five- to seven-year-old whiskey that was to bring a profit of $40,000 ("I do not believe there is another soul that has been able to get a contract the equal of the one I made"), but it never came to pass. He had not checked to find out what would happen after he bought the whiskey. ("I am concerned now how long before we can bring the goods into the States, what the tax will be, their wholesale and retail license costs and if there will be state and city taxes to pay. Besides, the government may control in some way the sale of the merchandise.") This list of unknowns, plus the absolute refusal of British distillers to consider any terms but cash, made it impossible for him to build his business in ways he had used in the past—with time and credit. He liquidated the company a few months into 1934, selling the whiskey he had left over to the Pick hotels at cost plus 10%. He had made a small profit in the venture.

He turned from whiskey to tomatoes, investing in a farm that was experimenting with hybrids, but he had no way of evaluating what was being done. In this venture he was less open with Gertrude. In fact, he told almost no one, though he told Albert he was "exploring new ventures" and later talked a little about the tomatoes to Albert and Corinne. But nothing more was known, not even how much money he lost in the brief exploration.

Albert, Jr., in Chicago, had little patience for his father's experiments, though he might have responded, if asked, that the money being used for them was hard-won by him on his father's behalf. He did not say so, however; he was absorbed in matters that ranged from keeping the lights on in empty hotel rooms to paying at least partial salaries so the company could retain its staffs to acting as the trustee of the two trust funds still belonging to his father and mother.

Monies, stocks, and bonds were being transferred from one trust to another by Albert, Sr. Albert, Jr., had paid $30,000 and given his note as trustee to exempt Gertrude from any enforcement of deficiency decrees. He also signed a promissory note, as trustee, for $55,000 to be paid in installments over two and a half years.

At the same time, two distant family members who owned stock in the Pick Hotels Corporation (none was ever sold to the public) became alarmed by the published reports of Albert, Sr.'s bankruptcy and made vague threats of litigation to protect their interests. Albert, Jr., feeling besieged but without an alternative as the sole protector of the family business, borrowed $30,000 to buy their shares in the company.

By 1937, facing a Board of Directors that had weathered the bankruptcy proceedings and the worst years of the depression with him, that had seen the slow growth of the business as hotels were acquired through foreclosures and repeal allowed hotel bars to begin making money, and that supported him totally through personal loyalty and trust in his financial judgment, he felt at last master in his house. It was time now to begin to build the structure he had been envisioning through the long difficult years.

9

The Pick Hotels Corporation

A T CHRISTMASTIME, 1942, Volume 1, Number 1, of *Topicks,* the magazine of the Pick Hotels, appeared, bearing a name chosen in a contest among employees, and flashing pictures of Albert Pick, Chairman of the Board, and Albert Pick, Jr., President, on the front cover.

The "Christmas message" was from Albert, Jr., the first in a stream of editorial comments that would continue until the 1970s, always appearing over his signature, always discussing the hotels, world issues, or his and Corinne's travels, as if he were writing to family members about the latest doings from his house to theirs. It was a style and an approach that would characterize everything he did in the hotel business. Today, some would call it naive; but if it was, it was the reflection of a more innocent time; and it probably contributed to the success of the hotel chain.

One of the first hotels in which he made the "family" approach a way of business was the Mark Twain—for a time the "flagship of the chain." This St Louis hotel had gone through a series of crises, first in its construction, when the original owner ran out of financing, and later when, barely opened for business, it faced the crash of 1929. Joseph Grand, one of the lawyers involved in all the phases of the hotel's life, including its sale to Albert, later described it as "snowed under with debts, defaulted bonds, and mechanics' liens."

Albert went to St. Louis in 1940, having heard through one of his lawyers, I. B. Lipson, that the hotel could be purchased. He met in what was recalled by Grand as a "mass meeting" with lawyers, receivers, and representatives of a number of local groups involved with the hotel. It was one of the first times he had faced a large group with proposals so intricate that they satisfied the objections of all members. Others commented on his forthrightness and knowledgeability in spite of comparative youth, and it was not long before the Mark Twain (soon renamed the Pick-Mark Twain) was his, and its "rebirth" began.

He knew, and soon others in the corporation knew, that the business community of St. Louis credited him with turning around a failing hotel. Not only had he added a money-making operation to his company, he had aided the stability of downtown St. Louis by, as Grand put it, turning a "rank failure . . . into a blossoming flower." It was a dual role he would try to emulate from then on.

By 1942, the chain held fifteen hotels in Indiana, Ohio, Missouri, Texas, and Kentucky, many bought under the same conditions of bankruptcy and chaos as prevailed with the Mark Twain. Most of the hotels were older buildings in the central sections of older cities that included: Cleveland, Columbus, Toledo, Cincinnati, Dayton, and Youngstown, Ohio; Indianapolis, Indiana; and St. Louis, Missouri. The Raleigh Hotel in Waco, Texas, had the patina of nostalgia; it had been the first owned by the Picks and was the one Albert, Jr., and Corinne had visited for their honeymoon—except for their snowbound week in the small, unheated inn they found when their car broke down.

Less than a year later, Albert began the move toward aggressive, often dramatic, purchases that would give the chain luster even when many of its properties were small and located in small towns. He heard that Lehman Brothers investment firm, and the General Realty and Development Corporation of New York, co-owners of the elegant Eldorado Towers apartments at 90th street and Central Park West, were looking for a buyer. Occupancy of the building was only 45%, rent control prevented the kind of profits the owners had anticipated when they bought, and a number of repairs were needed.

Albert had admired the building time and again on his trips to New York; its twin towers rising above the park were symbols to him of the sophistication of a most sophisticated city. Later, he would say he "thought it was worth twenty-five million dollars" (a sum he would not have paid for it); in fact, the asking price was two-and-a-half million and he paid it. He had, he said, "fallen in love with the building."

He named his top salesman from Chicago manager of the Eldorado and began his first saturation marketing campaign, running advertisements in the *Wall Street Journal* every morning for a month. Within four months, he had occupancy to the break-even point. When rent control was lifted, he increased rents across the board by fifteen percent, redecorated, upgraded the staff, and not only rented out the building, with a top rental for a fourteen-room apartment of $6,000/year, but had a waiting list as well.

Albert made what he later called "a fortune" on the Eldorado, but he sold it in four years to a buyer who was willing to pay five million dollars. The investment taught him a great deal: that his emotional attachment to a building, though evidently not a hindrance in making the decision to buy, had to be suppressed when a better offer came along. As simple as that sounded when he phrased it to himself, he had not acted according to it at some times in the past and, much later, would forget it again. (He had bought a motel in Colorado Springs, Colorado, because he "fell in love with" the view of Pike's Peak; when the rains came and the creek flooded and the building needed shoring up at great expense, he said he had learned that emotion wasn't a good basis for buying a piece of property.)

For the most part, he would buy and sell as circumstances dictated, zealously watching out for the welfare of employees caught in the buying and selling, but feeling little or no concern for the buildings themselves. There was one exception: the Pick-Congress in Chicago, but that hotel, and the circumstances surrounding it, was still in the future.

The hotel company's offices were in the Civic Opera Building, built by Samuel Insull in 1929, at a cost of 20 million dollars. The building stands next to the land once owned by Albert Pick, Sr., who, for a time, had the corner office in the Pick Hotels suite where his son was president and he was chairman of the board. At that time, in 1944, the home office staff numbered thirty-one people. Albert enjoyed the small group feeling, the sense that he was dealing with a family rather than a company. He liked and enjoyed working with Edgar Moss and Harold McCormick and the others who had been with him from the first. In the next two years, when the soldiers returned home and the chain began adding new hotels, the section of the newsletter devoted to news of individual hotels would be called "The Family Circle." (Albert had guaranteed soldiers jobs on their return if they had worked for the hotels before the war; he overstaffed by 10% for a year to make sure no one lost a job to make way for a returning soldier.)

Albert felt that anyone who worked for him and his company was part of an extended family that he had created to greet and care for travelers. He was the host; they were his staff. He and they stood ready in their "homes" to welcome strangers to make them comfortable, and to speed them on their way with hopes they would soon return.

It was not unrealistic, in light of the hotel atmosphere in Europe, described to him by other hotelmen and by his father and mother who had been to Europe a number of times. It was

Albert and Corinne
with Gladys, 1932

Three generations: Albert Pick, Sr.,
Albert Pick, Jr., and Albert III, 1937.

Center Portrait: ALBERT PICK SR., Chairman of the Board

L. E. BONE
Assistant
Gen'l Manager

O. E. TRONNES
Sales and Advertising
Manager

ALBERT PICK JR.
President

H. J. McCORMICK
Vice-President and
Gen'l Manager

WALTER
GREENHOLT
Asst. Treasurer

MORRISON
WORTHINGTON
Secretary

Officers of Albert Pick Hotels, 1936 (from a company publication)

Albert Pick, Sr., and Gertrude
Frank Pick in Miami Beach, 1929.

Nadine Van Sant, secretary
to Albert Pick, Jr., for
thirty-six years.

Gertrude Frank Pick Children's Center of La Rabida
Children's Hospital and Research Center, Chicago.

Albert Pick Hall for International Studies, The
University of Chicago, with the "Dialogo" sculpture by Virginio Ferrari.

Pick Staiger Concert Hall, Northwestern University, Evanston, Illinois (Lake Michigan in background).

Albert Pick Hall for International Studies, the University of Miami, with a Virginio Ferrari sculpture.

The family vacationing
in California in 1945.

Gertrude Frank Pick, 1942

Albert Pick, Jr., and his son, Albert III, 1950.

Albert, Gladys, Albert III and Corinne, 1948

From left, Richard J. Daley, Bob Hope, Albert Pick, Jr., Corinne Pick, Jack Benny and Irv Kupcinet gathering before a charitable gala held in the Pick-Congress Hotel, Chicago.

Albert and Corinne with Mr. and Mrs. Herbert Brownell in the Pick-Lee House, Washington, D.C., during inauguration ceremonies for the first term of President Dwight D. Eisenhower, 1952.

Albert Pick, Jr., and Dwight Eisenhower during the time when Albert was active in the People-to-People movement which Eisenhower had conceived and helped create.

not unrealistic, either, when seen as one expression of Albert's attitude toward people as opposed to institutions. Nowhere would this be more apparent than in his philanthropic activities, where he struggled constantly to deal with individuals, to arrange complicated matters with individuals, to give to individuals, when institutions always loomed up to intervene. In his hotels, he was determined to keep the entity of a company and the physical structures the company bought from assuming characteristics that would interfere with the relationships of individuals to each other: employee to fellow employee, employee to guest, employee to company executives, and executives to employees. Because he was sincere in this, with not a trace of hypocrisy, he was genuinely admired by employees who cared little for individual hotels but a great deal for Albert Pick, Jr.

They worked hard—and especially hard after the war. Business was good; in fact, business boomed. An air of freedom moved across the country as if the war had been a prison bottling emotions as well as mobility. Families took trips, explored America's sights and sounds, visited new cities. Business expanded; and conferences and conventions, held in abeyance for five years, were scheduled in a rush. Money was available and being spent; optimism and release made caution a strange word. Maybe later; not today.

For those who knew the business world, the postwar years were an ideal time to make money. Albert found new sets of figures on the books. The tight days of the '30s and the uncertain ones of the war seemed gone in a flurry of activity; peace and repeal together sent a quiver through the hotel world and, almost overnight, the horizons expanded.

For a time, Pick Hotels were adding at least one new hotel a year to the chain. The Georgian in Evanston, Illinois, just a few blocks from Northwestern University where Albert would one day build a concert hall as an anniversary gift to Corinne, was purchased in 1946; Pittsburgh's Roosevelt Hotel, in 1947;

the Melbourne in St. Louis and the Anderson in Anderson, Indiana, both in 1948. In 1950, the company completed renovation work on an apartment building—the Tower Apartments —that had stood empty for twenty years in Anderson, Indiana; it was one of the company's few ventures into apartments following the success of the Eldorado in New York.

The Georgian in Evanston was peculiarly bound up with the Pick family, and would be for years. Albert, Sr., had built it with "Dude" Paschen, a Chicago contractor; but, before the building was occupied, he sold out his interest to Paschen and the architect in a violent quarrel over construction costs. Albert, Jr., had been buying stock in the Georgian for some years when, in 1946, he finally acquired full control. Members of the family, including Hugo Pick and his wife, lived in the Georgian during the time Albert owned it; and Albert, Sr., himself, with Gertrude and Dorothy, often lived in the Georgian when they came to Chicago from Miami for the summers. It was an elegant building on a quiet, cool, tree-lined street in Evanston, with stately homes stretching to the south and, two blocks north, the expanding campus of Northwestern University. Albert loved the building; and, reflecting that, Lester Alwood, editor of *Topicks,* ran photographs and stories emphasizing its charm and old-world elegance.

But Albert's purchase had been the source of another quarrel with his father. Albert, Sr., had interpreted it as "a way to make money on my losses out of spite"; and, when Albert protested he had done it for his father, the argument ended abruptly, as so many others, with his father walking out and ignoring him for some weeks. Later, Albert would recall that he was "fed up" because of the quarrel; and when the Methodist Church came to him in 1962 with an offer to buy the hotel for an old people's home, he sold it. He made a profit of one million dollars on his investment, which revived his father's anger; and even Gertrude's attempts to patch things up failed until time achieved what she could not.

Albert's success with the hotel chain, which became a fact during and after the second world war, and in the next two decades, was the first signal success of the Pick family since the supply company had reached its peak in the mid-1920s. For a family of aggressive, driving, confident businessmen, it had been a long time. Albert, Sr., rebuilding his fortune in real estate and investment in a bank in Miami, watched from that distance his son build a wide-spread hotel chain with the name Pick in city after city, with revenues pouring in. As Albert traveled to Europe, where he took the Pick name to meetings of professional hoteliers, his father felt far off, out of the mainstream, and out of the sphere of influence he once had exerted over his son and other members of the family, all of whom had depended upon him for their living. He was in and out of Chicago (he had an office in the suite in the Civic Opera Building, though he did not have one when the company moved to larger quarters with an expanded staff), but there was no question that the Pick Hotels Corporation was Albert, Jr.'s company, all its stock held by him, all its decisions made by him, and a small group of trusted men with whom he was in daily contact when he wintered in Florida and on whom he relied when, later, he and Corinne took long trips to Europe and Asia.

Albert reveled in it: the control, the successes, the creation of a structured, visible company whose assets—buildings, people, reputation—he could see as the results of his financial skill and his staff's managerial talents. He was more at ease with his father than at any previous time in his life and was able to join with him in a number of real estate ventures in Florida, perhaps for the first time as a true equal. They were not close, but they had achieved a measure of mutual respect that lasted the rest of Albert, Sr.'s life.

The high point of Albert's hotel career came with the purchase of Chicago's Congress Hotel in 1950. He had been eyeing the Congress for some time. With the Stevens Hotel, which had been built by the family of John Paul Stevens (who would be appointed to the United States Supreme Court by President Gerald Ford) and later sold to become the Conrad Hilton Hotel, it dominated the skyline of South Michigan Avenue, at one time Chicago's most prestigious street. Later, North Michigan Avenue, beyond the Chicago River, would become the city's "magnificent mile," with the hotel names of Marriott, Continental Plaza, and Sheraton sitting snugly beside the most elegant names in haute couture. But in the early 1950s, South Michigan Avenue, wide, tree-lined, boasting the Art Institute on its east side and Orchestra Hall, home of the Chicago Symphony Orchestra, on the west, was a center of shopping, culture, and dining, and the Congress Hotel was one of its most impressive features.

Certainly, it was the most impressive building in the Pick hotel chain. A special issue of *Topicks* was devoted to it, lyricizing over its features, ranging from the Office of the Public Stenographer to the Glass Hat supper club at the end of "Peacock Alley," the wide corridor extending from the north to the south end of the block-long hotel. The murals in the lobby were reproduced, with captions explaining their content; the presidential suite (occupied by Senator Robert Taft during the presidential convention of 1952, in which Albert played a part) was shown in photographs of each room; the nine party rooms were described and illustrated; and the staff of the hotel was given its due in pictures and text. Even Buckingham fountain, Chicago's landmark across Michigan Avenue from the hotel, was described in detail, from the cost of erection to the one-and-a-half-million gallon central pool to the times at night when the color display was on view.

The Congress was a triumphant acquisition, the crown jewel of the Pick Hotels, and Albert and Corinne both felt about the hotel as they would about a brilliant child bringing renown to the family name. They entertained in the Congress—its name became the Pick-Congress upon acquisition—and watched with delight as organizations from the political to the religious to the social chose its facilities for conventions and meetings. Even the Columbia Broadcasting System chose the Pick-Congress in 1962, using it as the site for its "Years of Crisis" panel discussion before an audience in the Gold Room.

The acquisition of the Congress was one of the milestones to which Albert later pointed when tracing the growth of the hotel chain. There were others, some quiet, some dramatic, some his own ideas, some borrowed from different hotel chains (Albert and Conrad Hilton sat on several committees together, and he was an active participant and leader in national and international hotel associations); but in all of them, small and large, he took a close, intense interest.

One event which used the Pick name and hotel renown to achieve publicity that became the talk of Chicago and made other hotelmen envious for months to come was staged by Albert and the Pfaelzer brothers at the 1953 International Livestock Exhibition at the Chicago Stockyards. Monroe and Ellard Pfaelzer, owners of one of the country's largest meat-packing firms, were Albert's friends of many years' standing, and he trusted their business judgment. When Monroe called him one day and asked him to participate in the annual auction held by the 4-H Club, he asked a few questions, thought it sounded like harmless fun, if nothing better, and went out to the Stockyards.

The animal to be auctioned, a massive white-faced steer named Lone Star, was described as weighing over one thousand pounds. The bidding began at $12 a pound (live weight); at $17.50, all bidders but Albert and Ed Pollack of the Drake Hotel on Chicago's Michigan Avenue dropped out. The two men continued to bid; Albert was bidding through Monroe. At $18 a pound Monroe told Albert to go up to $20. "It will break all records for steer prices, and I have the publicity all ready to go. It will be a lulu."

Albert, caught up in the bidding, nodded. Pollack dropped

out, and Lone Star became the property of the Pick Hotels. The weighmaster presented Albert with the bill and a blank check. Albert looked at both and looked at Lone Star. "How do I know how much he really weighs?" he asked.

The weighmaster showed him the certificate of weight as 1,055 pounds. Albert thought a moment, then shook his head. "That steer was weighed six hours ago. He hasn't had any food; he's been walking around urinating in the hot kleig lights. I want him weighed again."

Expostulations about tradition at the Stockyards were no good; Albert wanted an official weighing before he wrote the check. And when Lone Star was weighed, it was found he'd lost fifty pounds in the six hours of auction and Stockyards festivities. Albert wrote a check for $20,000—and got what Fairfax Cone, his advertising friend, called "publicity that a million dollars couldn't have bought" in all the Chicago newspapers and on wire services across the country.

In addition, he got a number of special rib roasts from Lone Star, the first two of which went to President and Mrs. Eisenhower, and the second two, to Governor and Mrs. Stratton of Illinois. At the same time, he bought a prize load of cattle to send beef to all the hotels in the chain, whose menus then listed steaks and other servings as "from the prize load."

Another, more serious but no less pleasant event, also of considerable news value, was the Albert Pick Centennial of 1957. Strictly speaking, the company had not been a hotel chain for one hundred years; but Albert held a gala celebration of "100 years of service to hoteldom" which was in fact the case, and added, to make the issue more immediate, "America's oldest hotel family."

The centennial luncheon was held for 250 guests in the Golden Room of the Pick-Congress. Albert used the occasion to gather in one place the leading business, industrial, and political figures in Chicago. In addition, he had matchbooks and souvenir folders manufactured for distribution to staff in all the hotels. The occasion became a birthday party for everyone, with Albert the proud father, presiding and beaming with pleasure beneath the carved, vaulted ceiling and heavy chandeliers of his Gold Room.

But the centennial, dramatic as it was, did not represent the kind of business milestones Albert counted when measuring the success of the chain. He did not have, as examples, the kinds of daring plunges his father had made over the years; but he could point to movement, growth and expansion after careful study and with as many precautions as anyone in business could take. He had failures, many unavoidable; but, over the life of the hotel chain, he took pride in the number of successful moves he had made and the quality of the company he had built.

In 1955, for the first time, the company grew from "Albert Pick Hotels" to "Albert Pick Hotels and Motor Inns." American travel habits were changing, and it was clearly time to enter the motel business. "Instead of competing with themselves by so doing," he wrote in *Topicks,* "hotel-chain operators in the motel field are able not only to complement their downtown operations but to provide the same fine service standards for other localities as well."

Rather than trying to dominate the field, Albert moved into it by joining with another company: he made a four-million-dollar leasing arrangement with Holiday Inns of America to lease and operate ten Holiday Inns. The first two, by the time the announcement was made in November, 1955, were already open in Natchez, Mississippi, and Colorado Springs, Colorado. Three others soon would be opened, in Terre Haute, Indiana, and Nashville and Chattanooga, Tennessee. Later, he built and bought his own motels, moving away from the connection with Holiday Inns.

Motel management, he found, was not foreign to a hotel management team. The difficulties came with factors beyond his expertise or control. A major highway would be re-routed, as happened in Atlanta, and the inevitable plummeting of business forced him to sell. In Mobile, he was the first on the street to build a motor inn; others followed and overbuilt so that, in a few years, he was the first to sell and leave the area.

But these were expected fluctuations of the business. The peak number of forty-one hotels and motels lasted only a short time; the average over twenty years of innkeeping was closer to thirty, with locations and hotel and motel names shifting with the passing years. On the whole, he was satisfied with the motels in the chain; in some, he took great pride—among them, the two-hundred-seventy-five room Nationwide Inn in Columbus, Ohio, with a convention hall seating five hundred and small private rooms. "A defining line between hotels and motels," he said in 1959, "generally speaking, no longer exists today." The truth of that observation was due in no small part to Albert's role in upgrading the quality of motels in downtown and edge-of-town locations and making them hotels to the traveler.

Long before he turned his attention to colleges and universities as focal points of faith in the future, Albert was concerned about young people who needed to find niches for themselves in the world as badly as business and society needed to have those niches filled. He spoke often of the problems facing youngsters who could not afford an extensive education, and he foresaw the tightening job market that would plague America some years later, sending many who *had* been able to manage the extensive education into areas for which they had no training or inclination, simply because there was no work in their chosen fields.

In addition, he was concerned about the future of hotels. He knew that there never were enough good workers for the jobs that had to be done. It was not his nature to castigate or to chide—he often was criticized, in fact, for being too "soft" on employees who needed reprimanding—but he knew, from looking for good points to praise, how few good points there often were. In a sense, he felt responsible for the future of privately-owned hotels in America as, later, he would feel at least partially responsible for relations between people in countries around the world. That sense of responsibility would underlie the choices he made in his philanthropic activities and the time and energy he gave to the national People to People organization and professional hotel associations.

For now, in 1958, he moved in the area of his greatest concern in those years—the future of hotels—and established a program to pay for one hundred Pick Hotels' employees each year to enroll in a home study course under the direction of the American Hotel Institute. In his editorial in the issue of *Topicks* explaining the program, he wrote, "In line with our policy of steady and intelligent expansion, the question of constant and serious concern to us is that of *whom* we can select from our own ranks to occupy bigger and better-paying positions in our chain of hotels and motels as the occasion arises."

On the facing page of the same issue was reprinted a column on hotels by Herb Graffis of the Chicago *Sun-Times* which described "the reservation system at these icy, gigantic barracks [which] offers the guest the same sort of welcome you imagine a lifer gets."

> There are schools [Graffis went on] training young men for the honorable profession of sheltering the roaming citizens. This schooling must be good, but it seems to have frozen out the learning the hotel men used to get from customers. At many hotels now you get the impression the place is run for the book-keepers and stockholders, and if the guests don't like it, let them stay away.

Albert was determined that no hotel or motel bearing his name would ever meet that description. The free training program was a natural step for him, and one he would recall as a "natural investment in the future."

He was involved as well in investing in a different segment of the hotel industry: helping to create scholarships for universities that gave degrees in hotel management, including Cornell and Michigan State, and for the Culinary Institute in New Haven, Connecticut (later moved to New York state). He had given funds to the Culinary Institute since its founding in 1946, first as an admirer of Frances Roth, who began the school as a place to turn veterans of World War II into chefs and restaurant managers, later as a supporter of the excellence of the institution, which had grown to one of the finest in the country. In 1964, the institute staff recognized his support, both personal and through the American Hotel and Motel Association, by naming a new student dormitory on its campus the Albert Pick, Jr., Hall.

It was yet another kind of investment when he reorganized the hotel company in 1960, separating the motels into their own division and naming Edgar Moss, who had been with him since 1939, Executive Vice-President and General Manager of both the hotel and the motel divisions. Pick Dining, Inc., the industrial dining division, managed restaurants and cafeterias separate from the hotel and motel chain. The company was growing, not only in the number of properties it owned, but in the manner in which it operated; there was an increased knowledge of the vagaries of the hotel industry, of clients and customers, of employees, and of the uses of advertising. Along with this, or as part of it, came the feeling, in the prosperous mid-1960s, that expansion from the midwest and east coast was not only desirable, but necessary for financial stability and the image the company should project.

And so, in October 1964, the corporation added to its thirty-five hotels and motels the Lord Simcoe Hotel, in Toronto, and the Windsor Hotel, in Montreal, Canada. Under a franchise agreement with the general manager of the two hotels, the Pick Hotels referral and reservation networks were expanded into Canada; and for the first time the Corporation could say it had "gone international."

The next logical step was to straddle the United States, which the corporation did in May 1965, with a contract to operate the Caravan Inn in Sacramento, California. At the same time, a new motel in Atlanta was added on a long-term lease basis, and the Pleasant Point Resort in Point Pleasant, West Virginia, came in under a franchise agreement. The total number of properties in the chain—it was now at its peak—was forty-one hotels and motels in thirty-six cities in the United States and Canada.

Two years before the gala centennial celebration in 1957, Albert had editorialized on the silver anniversary of Pick Hotels. Tracing the Corporation from its beginnings under his father in 1926, with a staff of four people, to the current staff of fifty and a service personnel of nearly 5,000, he summed up:

> We have survived the disastrous depression days of the '30s, and the abnormal pressures and problems of World War II. We have maintained a conservative but steady policy of expansion; we have constantly and consistently improved our properties; we have contributed substantially to the civic and economic welfare of the communities in which we operate; and we enjoy today both a reputation for good service with the traveling public, and the cooperative good will of our fellow hotelmen, that are assets beyond price. We have, in short, come far and done well since those 'humble beginnings' of a quarter century ago.

The distance from the "humble beginnings" had been even more important to him because of the closeness of those who had been with him all the way. Prominent among these was his secretary and executive assistant, Nadine Van Sant, thirty-six years by his side, and later as much a family member as a corporate employee. His attorney and cousin, Alan Altheimer, who was married to his cousin, was another to whom he could turn as the years went by; and he later would say that it was the people "in his care" who meant the most to him.

Ten years later, when the chain had become "international" and "coast to coast" and had reached its peak in size, Albert felt even farther from these humble beginnings. His reputation as a businessman was secure in America and, through the International Hotel Association, in Europe. He was widely admired for charm and quiet wit and for the good sense to have married Corinne, who had long since been the Pick Hotels' best representative. The two were feted wherever they went, not, it seems, from protocol or the feathering of nests, but because they were genuinely liked. Casual, unpretentious, enthusiastic, with a disarming combination of youthful naivete and wordly sophistication, they embodied some of the best of that elusive entity called "American" before the prefix "ugly" was attached to it. They were at home in the small towns of America and the banquet halls of Europe, secure in their wealth and confident in their ability, but often modest in their behavior and visibly delighted at signs of acceptance and affection from others. It was a time, truly, of Albert's coming of age, on his own, in his own company, with the knowledge, when he traveled in America and Europe, that when the name Albert Pick, Jr., was announced, there was no confusion: the warm response was to him, as the representative of a country, a business, and a family.

He was traveling much of the time, both at home and abroad and, as always, spending winters in Florida. At one time, he and Corinne regularly had toured the hotels and motels that bore his name, checking on physical facilities, finances, personnel, and services. As the chain grew, he expanded his staff and let the new divisional managers and executives in the home office assume the supervision and financial planning he had controlled since the beginning. For almost four decades, he had built and run the largest privately owned hotel chain in America; by the early 1960s, nearly 70 years old, he had let the management and supervision pass to the hands of others.

Toward the end of the decade, in 1967, it was clear that the hotels had begun to slip. Maintenance, repairs, redecorating, advertising, training of personnel, all had been delayed or canceled; the balance sheets, which Albert did review regularly, showed a healthy, prosperous company; but the figures were unrealistic. To reach those rosy figures, too much was left undone.

When Albert became aware of the extent of the problem, he faced two alternatives: to sell the chain, or to reshape it to the image he held in his memory from earlier years. In the end, he held on. "Quite frankly," he wrote in his monthly editorial in 1969, "I will tell you that a few of our properties of the vintage years presented problems in this progressive age, where the main competition consists of brand new structures. . . . We were faced with a momentous decision as to whether to sell the older establishments or allocate millions of dollars to rehabilitate them. . . ."

The decision was made, he wrote, to allocate over five million dollars "to modernizing and glamourizing our properties, among which are the Pick-Carter, Cleveland; Pick-Roosevelt, Pittsburgh; Pick-Nicollet, Minneapolis; Pick-Durant in Flint, Michigan . . . the Pick-Fort Hayes Hotel in Columbus, Ohio; and the Albert Pick Motel in Nashville, Tennessee."

In addition, he took the occasion to announce the opening of a three-hundred-room motel in Memphis, Tennessee, a two-hundred-fifty-room high-rise motor inn in Houston, Texas, and the anticipated opening, a year hence, of a motel in South Bend, Indiana. "We are enthusiastic, excited and extremely optimistic over the future prospects of our company," he concluded, "and you, the executives and staff members, and all employees will share our pride in this revival—yes, in the rejuvenation of our chain."

His enthusiasm was real, though dimmed; he was genuinely concerned. The chain had been left to drift while his attention was on travel, the People to People movement, and hotel associations both national and international. He was not sure he could bring it back to health; he knew it was more than a question of money, that it would take supervision, energy, the kind of intense follow-through he had managed without a second thought when he was twenty years younger. Now he was close to 75; and, while he felt well and still enthusiastic about the world he and Corinne explored anew each year, he recognized the difficulty of climbing back to the heights the hotels had attained before.

But he saw no alternative. Two events, one small but merry, the other a significant decision, undergirded his decision to try to rejuvenate the chain. One was the triumph of the Pick-Congress in a prestigious, if little known, contest. The International Wine and Food Society, with headquarters in London and branches in ninety-seven cities around the world, had held its international convention in the Gold Room of the Pick-Congress in 1967, and Chef Amato Ferrero and Catering Manager D. Michael Jeans had received awards for the dinner. Two years later, the year in which Albert made the decision to "rejuvenate" rather than sell, the Chicago chapter presented its prestigious "Dinner of the Year" award to the Pick-Congress for the second time (the first had been in 1962). There would be a third award, but this small triumph, coming when it did gave Albert enormous pleasure, a metaphor, almost, for the sheer fun and satisfaction he gained from his hotels.

The other event, larger and more momentous, had taken place earlier. It represented a commitment that Albert, and Corinne as well, remembered keenly through the years. Lawrence Kimpton, former president of the University of Chicago and close friend of Albert and Corinne, had left the university for the Standard Oil Company. It was he who went to Albert as spokesman when the oil company wanted to buy the Pick-Congress Hotel. Standard Oil wanted a new building in Chicago to replace the one on South Michigan Avenue not far from the Pick-Congress; the decision had been made to remain downtown, and one of the most attractive and spacious corners was at Michigan and Congress (the latter by then was a major thoroughfare leading west through the center of the huge Chicago Post Office building into the Congress Expressway, now the Eisenhower Expressway). Standard Oil's plan was to tear down the Pick-Congress and build a new office building of Italian marble to gleam whitely above the city. Kimpton went to Albert with an offer of fifteen million dollars for his hotel.

Albert turned him down. When Kimpton smiled and said, "All right, Albert, how much?" Albert shook his head. He simply did not want to sell the Congress. But then he thought about it, doubted for a moment, and asked Corinne. She did not hesitate. They both loved it, she said; it had been their jewel for over ten years. Why should they sell it? The chain was doing well; the Congress always did them proud in terms of revenue and reputation. It made no sense to give up something they both loved, and that symbolized to them the Albert Pick Hotels at their best.

So they kept the Pick-Congress. Later, when he became too ill to cope with the problems of rejuvenation, Albert would regret the decision. But at the time, it was a statement by both him and Corinne that the business was going to stay in their hands, all of it, from the crown jewel in Chicago to the small Albert Pick "Hotella" in Miami Beach built by Albert, Sr. And that commitment weighed in the decision of 1969 to pour five million dollars into bringing an ailing business back to good health.

He had said he would try. That was the greatest commitment he could make.

10

La Rabida and the Children

L A RABIDA Sanitarium stands in solitary grandeur in Jackson Park on the south side of Chicago, a replica of a Spanish monastery, circa 100 A.D., within sight and/or sound of a multi-lane highway along Lake Michigan, commuter railroads, baseball players, and the wail of police and fire sirens that mark modern urban life.

The anomalies of La Rabida extend to its history. The replica built as the Spanish exhibition for the gaudy spectacle of the World's Columbian Exposition of 1893 became, almost immediately after the last crowds had left, a summer haven for the sick children of Chicago's poor. Later, with gifts of money from some of the city's wealthiest families, the building opened its doors and facilities to victims of rheumatic fever, most of them from neighborhoods of the city where there was no money for medicine or doctors, where, in fact, many of the residents had never seen the rest of the city or Lake Michigan. Financed with a devotion that was almost fanatical by the fund-raising activities of a women's board, it was managed, and all the major decisions were made by, the men of the Board of Trustees, of which Albert Pick, Jr., would become president.

By the 1950s, La Rabida had become one of the outstanding hospitals in the world for research in and treatment of rheumatic heart disease in children. Its greatness lay in the number of highly qualified and dedicated people who worked as volunteers for its continuance, the staff, and the Board of Trustees, headed by Albert Pick, Jr., who was later recalled as a man of broad visions with "the ability of the wealthy to delegate authority and think big."

A new building had been built in 1932, the original one having burned down ten years earlier, with Spanish-style architecture to warrant the retention of the name La Rabida. The women's board raised half a million dollars in 1929—no mean feat, and they knew it—for the new building; in the process, the board learned how to use the media (a word not widely in use in those days) for publicity: Isaac Gershman, managing editor of the City News Bureau in Chicago (whose son, not yet born, would one day be a patient at La Rabida) sent the story to 5,000 newspapers in the United States. Richard Finnegan, editor of the Chicago *Daily Times,* gave the story wide and continuous publicity in the city. Volunteer work and public speeches were provided by such luminaries as Judge Kenesaw Mountain Landis (who had made his colorful name even more colorful by imposing a hefty fine on Standard Oil of Indiana in a rebate case in 1907), Judge Henry Horner, and Lorado Taft (who was vice chairman of the campaign committee, a man close to the end of his life who was a kind of culture hero to the people of Chicago who talked of his sculptures as if they were neighbors). J. Roscoe Miller, one day to be a close friend of Albert Pick, Jr., was on the first advisory board—a board that, when the money was raised and the building constructed, without dissent asked Dr. Robert Black, then head of Loyola University's Department of Pediatrics, to be Director of La Rabida.

Robert Black had not so many years before carried his medical bags on house calls to, among many others, the home of Albert Pick, Sr. He came most often for Laurence, whose

damaged heart—from an early bout with rheumatic fever—
caused concern from his youngest years. But Dr. Black was also
a friend of the family and could share their fears with them.
He too had had rheumatic fever as a child; he too knew the
pain and the terror of an ailing heart. No one, in those days,
could know that Robert Black and Albert, Jr., who carried the
memory of his brother Laurence all his life, would work together on a hospital for rheumatic heart children that became
for both of them a cause and a kind of revelation. "It is the
most important of all my charities," Albert would say; and
he demonstrated this with time and energy, as well as money.

It was through Robert Black that Albert first heard of La
Rabida. Black had been active in the Sanitarium's earlier
versions; when the new building was opened in 1932, he left
Loyola to become its full-time director. The Sanitarium had
thirty beds at the time, and a long waiting list of patients.
The day-to-day operations were under the women's board, for
everything from purchasing food and supplies to presiding over
coffee and sandwiches on visiting day. A Building Committee
was in charge of buildings and grounds; the Investigating
Committee organized admitting and discharge functions; the
Ways and Means Committee raised money, especially collect-
ing on unpaid pledges promised the building drive (though,
by that time, the sanitarium was fully paid for); and the Board
of Trustees invested the money.

For all the efforts, the economy in the 1930s was a daunting
barrier to fundraisers. The sanitarium grew slowly, hampered
by lack of proper equipment and a forced stinginess with
supplies. In 1937, the La Rabida Foundation, an Illinois not-
for-profit corporation, was formed by the men's board (the
Board of Trustees) to help the women's board raise funds,
specifically, at the time, to open the second floor, adding beds
and lowering the cost per child (then $1.35 per patient per
day).

Robert Black gave the fundraisers their ammunition: 3,000

cardiac cases among the 60,000 children entering school each year; 75% of them curable with proper care; La Rabida alone in providing that care; capacity of the sanitarium could be 100 beds if fully expanded. The fund drive, with Mary Black, wife of Robert Black, as executive secretary, was aimed at $105,000 for three years' maintenance.

The drive was begun with a banquet at the Palmer House, at which Freddie Bartholomew, one of America's favorite child stars, spoke by telephone from Hollywood. That talk, together with the recorded and amplified sound of the beating of a sick child's damaged heart, made the drive one of the most successful in all that La Rabida held, and the sanitarium was on a firm financial footing, perhaps for the first time.

Eleanor Roosevelt wrote about La Rabida in her column "My Day"; but during the Second World War, the Sanitarium was in financial trouble again—the building needed major repairs, costs of day-to-day operation were rising rapidly, and fundraising was even more difficult during the war effort than it had been during the depression. In 1944, with the problems mounting, a new era began at La Rabida that was to involve Albert Pick, Sr., his son, and a number of others whose activities would be entwined with theirs for the rest of their lives.

J. Roscoe Miller, then Dean of the Northwestern University Medical School, and later the University's president, became Medical Coordinator of La Rabida; and the four medical schools in Chicago—the University of Chicago, Loyola, Northwestern, and the University of Illinois—agreed to rotate among themselves on three-year terms responsibility for the supervision of La Rabida's patients. Each school appointed medical advisory, attending, adjunct, and consulting staffs, an arrangement that was to last for thirteen years.

The same year, 1944, saw the beginning of the tenure of Richard Finnegan, editor of the Chicago *Daily Times*, as president of the Board of Trustees. It was to be a love afair that lasted until his death. He became passionately involved with the work of the sanitarium, the children who spent a day, a month, three months there before going home, and the staff in its medical and research activities.

Finnegan was a quiet, gentle man, recalled years after his death for a compassion rare in newspaper men who had worked the dark streets of Chicago. He had made his reputation on his brilliant coverage of the Eastland disaster; luck put him on the bridge over the Chicago River when the ship went down with 600 people, and he followed the story for days, building a name for careful, colorful, human reporting that avoided the saccharin but, it was said, made readers weep.

But from the scope of the Eastland disaster, Finnegan slipped easily into the smallness of La Rabida. The sanitarium seemed to lend itself to those who needed an intimate, closely held institution. Robert and Mary Black, it was reported, ran La Rabida as if it were their own fiefdom. They ran it with love and hard work that surpassed all expectations; but nonetheless, they ran it, with the adoring support of the women's board, as they saw fit.

Finnegan, too, treated the sanitarium as if it was his. He doted on its successes, worried through the nights over its problems, paced the floor over its failures. When he recruited for the staff, he did so as if taking the measure of candidates for his own family. And indeed, it was his family. When he died, La Rabida research was a major beneficiary of his estate and, from his hospital bed, one of the last things he did was make sure of his successor: Albert Pick, Jr.

But before that time, much happened to La Rabida. Its progress accelerated beyond what anyone could have predicted, due to Finnegan's driving energy and love for the institution and the Board of Trustees that worked with him, often in response to the heat of his enthusiasm. Albert Pick, Jr., was not yet as involved with La Rabida as he would be a decade later; but he admired what he saw there in the mid- and late 1940s, especially the dedication of the staff, and he assiduously did his part as a member of the board. Occasionally, he did more. When Franklin Roosevelt died on April 12, 1945, Albert wrote a letter the next day to Richard Finnegan, speaking of the late President's humanitarianism: "First and last, he was the friend and champion of the needy, the downtrodden, the defenseless minorities of the world. . . ." It was a posture Albert admired and, indeed, aspired to, since the early days of caring for Laurence. With the letter to Finnegan, he enclosed a check for $1,000 to perpetually endow a bed at La Rabida in memory of Roosevelt.

The 50th anniversary of La Rabida was celebrated in 1946, and the staff was talking about a radical change in the structure of the hospital. Until then, it had been a place for the convalescence of children ill with rheumatic heart disease and other diseases often caused by poor nutrition and squalid living conditions. Now, the Chief of Staff, Dr. William Elghammer, saw his, and the hospital's responsibility as providing "material for the intensive research into the cause, the nature and the treatment of rheumatic fever and rheumatic heart diseases in children."

The subject was debated for the next few years—how best to fund and provide an ongoing program of research. The climate was changing in the country. Medical research following the war was expanding at a furious pace, with money coming from the government for the first time in significant amounts. Research had a glamor combined with a mystical aura of saving lives in the laboratory that reached a peak of popularity after so many lives had been lost on the battlefield. Then, in 1949, cortisone was discovered, and the treatment of a number of heretofore crippling diseases was altered forever.

It was a watershed year for many institutions, La Rabida among them. Richard Finnegan, already active on the Chicago Heart Council, put his authority as Chairman of the Board of La Rabida behind the full-scale introduction of research at the hospital. He brought in a new Chief of Staff and Medical

Director, Dr. Hugh McCulloch, former chief pediatrician in charge of the rheumatic fever program of the Missouri State Services for Crippled Children, and editor-in-chief of the medical journal *Pediatrics.*

McCulloch began using cortisone at La Rabida and instituted bi-weekly conferences with the families of patients in a new program of home service and education. At the same time, through the volunteers at the hospital, he created a program of "foster mothers" for hospitalized children. In 1950, a research laboratory was built in the basement of La Rabida.

If Albert connected the children and the increasingly complex activities of La Rabida with the beloved brother who had died of the effects of rheumatic heart disease, he did not speak about it to those around him. But he watched the growth of the institution and the way its fame was spreading, evidenced by the number of doctors who came from Mexico, Latin America, and Europe to study the routine, diet, exercises, medication, and other elements of the care of convalescing children. He strongly supported the change, in 1949 and the years following, to a research hospital with facilities for surgery (La Rabida's first tonsillectomy was performed in 1950) and the treatment, rather than simply the care during convalescence, of seriously ill children. He was especially gratified when, at the end of 1950, the hospital research staff, headed by Albert Dorfman of the University of Chicago, was chosen as one of the members of an international team studying the long term, and possible preventive, effects of cortisone and ACTH on rheumatic fever and heart disease.

He had given money over many years, including the F. D. R. endowment and another thousand dollars he had given in 1944 to honor his father's 75th birthday. In a sense, Albert, Sr., opened the way for grander gestures (though how much his gift was chosen because of Albert's position on the Board of Trustees and his earlier gifts was never known). Though he had had little to do with the sanitarium until then, Albert, Sr., gave $300,000 for the Gertrude Frank Pick Children's Center a few years after the death of his wife; the memorial was dedicated on December 12, 1953, with the mayor of Chicago cutting the ribbons and Albert, Sr.'s granddaughter Gladys (Albert, Jr.'s daughter) unveiling the portrait of Gertrude Frank Pick in the entrance hall.

What was not publicly known for some time was that Albert, Jr., also had made a gift for the memorial to his mother. He and his father were at a particularly bad time in their stormy relationship, and he told friends that, had his father known he was joining in the gift, the building would never have been built; his father would have withdrawn his contribution. The two men never discussed it, so it is not certain that Albert, Sr., would have reacted so strongly, but, in any event, Albert, Jr.'s gift of a carillon and a pledge of $50,000 to be paid at $10,000 per year for five years' maintenance of the Gertrude Frank Pick Memorial Building was made quietly, with no fanfare.

The building became the Outpatient Department and the center of the Home Care Service, at that time serving over a thousand children. The service acted as a bridge between the hospital where the children had been living for varying amounts of time and their homes, neighborhoods, and schools. Classrooms, recreation facilities, and rehabilitation programs provided outpatient care as well as preparation for children to take part in the routines of the outside world. Albert, Jr., was sometimes seen there, watching the small patients prepare to return home, cured or well on their way; in some of them, perhaps, he saw Laurence, and himself as well, in the days when he carried Laurence's medication to school and fought as his protector in the playground.

He was becoming absorbed by the hospital, as were most who spent time there. Its small size and close-knit staff, the desperately sick children brought in by parents who looked upon doctors and nurses as gods who would perform miracles for them and their children, the warmth of the volunteers whose dedication was a reflection of their own needs for caring and being needed, all led once indifferent or casual businessmen to become emotional and as dedicated as the volunteers.

Later, Albert, Jr., was remembered as one who had "broader visions" than Richard Finnegan. Finnegan himself might have agreed; Albert's wealth, his world travels, his experiences with the volatile life of his father, all gave him a sophistication that allowed him to look far ahead. Like Daniel Burnham, he did not believe in making "little plans." When Finnegan died, having first made sure that Albert would take over as president of La Rabida, Albert made his first move, one he had been contemplating for some time: an alliance between La Rabida and the University of Chicago.

It was a natural alliance in many ways. La Rabida was not far from the university; the two institutions represented a unity of purpose as well as geography in their dedication to research, learning, and laying a groundwork for the future in the well-being of young people. In addition, Albert Dorfman, of the University of Chicago staff, already was Research Director of La Rabida—commuting from one position to the other—and the University of Chicago was one of the four universites participating in the staffing of La Rabida on a rotating basis.

The idea was not new. As far back as 1940, Dr. Black had attempted to gain university affiliation—at the time, La Rabida had no research program of its own—but at that time and again in 1942, when William Burton, vice-president of the university, and Dr. Morris Fishbein, of La Rabida's Board of Trustees, tried again, the university seemed indifferent. In fact, it was probably the case that it was not indifferent but alarmed. During the war years—as during most years in its history—there was little sentiment for adding another institution with its own large budget that would be a drain on the budget of the university.

A few years later, Richard Finnegan asked Lowell Cogges-hall, Dean of the university's Division of Biological Sciences, to reopen the question of affiliation; it was partly in response to that "reminder" that La Rabida expanded to include basic research with Albert Dorfman the Director, but the matter of affiliation got no further.

By the time Albert, Jr., became president of La Rabida, affiliation was more than desirable; it was urgently necessary. Federal research grants were going to universities but not to small private hospitals, and La Rabida's fundraising efforts were no longer enough to support its multiple functions. Until recently, the hospital had been free to all patients. Under Finnegan, a plan of payment according to the parents' ability to pay had been instituted; and also during his tenure, support was provided by the University of Illinois Division of Services for Crippled Children and the Variety Club of Illinois (which, from the mid-1940s on, gave over one million dollars to La Rabida). But if the research program was to grow without serious constraints, and more children be cared for every year as awareness of the hospital brought new families with their children, a continuing, stable flow of funds had to be achieved, partly through government research grants and partly through its place within the structure of the University of Chicago.

Albert was strongly committed to affiliation. He knew from his own company, and his father's before that, that a point had been reached in La Rabida's growth requiring some change in its structure to prevent it from stagnating. Its influence and prestige were international, but that was still largely from its work in the treatment of children suffering from rheumatic heart disease; it was not in the forefront of research. Funds and the stature of the university were needed, and Albert moved to realize both.

He had the support of Lawrence Kimpton, chancellor of the university; and, through Kimpton, he became friendly with and gained the support of Lowell Coggeshall. The three men, together with Albert Dorfman, testified to the excellence of La Rabida's teaching and service, arguing against the university's Board of Trustees' reluctance to assume the burden of the hospital's growing budget. Had the argument been carried by less than these four strong-willed and positive men, affiliation probably would not have been gained.

As it was, the arguments toppled the objections. It was especially important to the university's Board of Trustees that La Rabida not only had a history of superb teaching but also a wide reputation as a place matched by few other institutions for type of service and quality of staff. So it was that, at a luncheon attended by Albert Pick, Jr., Lawrence Kimpton, and Lowell Coggeshall, final agreements were reached, with the approval of the trustees. And on July 1, 1957, the university assumed full responsibility for care, teaching, and research at the new La Rabida-University of Chicago Institute. Albert Dorfman was named the overall director, and Burton Grossman was named the medical director.

Generally, it was a heady time for Albert. He was recognized as the architect of the affiliation (because Dr. Black, who had died in 1952, had been on the staff of the Loyola Medical School, many had thought affiliation, had it come about, would have been with that university) and he was moving in circles that stimulated him. He was remembered much later as one who enjoyed meeting and working with presidents of institutions and high officers of corporations.

Albert had known all his life the things money could buy and the sense of power that was a part of giving money to others. In fact, he seemed anxious to give money, and it is probable that power was only one aspect of his giving. He was later called a "soft touch," responsive to casual acquaintances, long-time friends, large institutions and small ones. Once, on a plane, he met a political scientist who talked of a research trip he could not make for lack of funds, and he gave the man a check, then and there, to take a sabbatical and do his research.

Another time, Albert Dorfman was planning a European trip with his wife, and Albert gave him a loan of $500. When Dorfman tried to repay it later, Albert was hurt and angry; he had thought they both understood it was a gift.

Giving, he thought, should always be personal. The remote request, the mailed check perhaps had their place; but, in his lexicon, the outstretched hand had more meaning, and he wanted to be able not only to put money in that hand but to shake it as well, to put his arm around the shoulders of the needy, and to assure them that he would do what he could.

There certainly was the sense of power, but there also seemed to be a search for love and acceptance—and admiration. He was not, even at this good time in his life (in his early sixties, vigorous, good looking, successful in his company, in love with his wife) a relaxed man. He found it difficult to unbend and become "one of the boys." Photographs of him at this time show him standing in a boat, poling, or, muscles strained, in a bowling alley, about to let go of the ball, but wearing a suit and tie, perhaps, though not invariably, with the jacket unbuttoned. He knew what was proper, and he could not change it to match more casual times. The image of his father—ramrod straight, narrow shoulders held back, head up and slightly tilted, aloof—was always in his mind.

Then, too, he had been the president or director of large corporations for a long time, with hundreds of people looking to him for direction and example. Corinne contributed to his self image as well; she deferred to him in matters assumed to be beyond her province—financial, business, dealing with real estate—and, in general, made him feel that the family, as well as the hotels he owned and the people who staffed them, circulated around him.

In any case, there was a place where he was rewarded with respect and a portion of awe (though Corinne never disappointed him by withholding those at home). He visited La Rabida frequently and was greeted by the staff as a "great man," as a staff member recalled. They knew he was interested in them; regular, frequent visits and a steady stream of money donated to one part of the institution or another, as well as gifts of goods, testified to that. He had given a mink coat and muff to be raffled off, and an automobile; he endowed beds whenever there was an occasion; he prevailed upon his friend the comedian Bob Hope to come for a La Rabida benefit; he led the fund drive for the Richard J. Finnegan Memorial Building and Variety Club Research Center; he loaned money to the women's board for fixtures and stock for a gift shop in the Pick Building of La Rabida; and he had donated $25,000 for the Laurence Mercer Pick Memorial Library at La Rabida.

"Some wealthy people," a friend said years later, "won't give a cent to causes or institutions; some give all at once in a chunk. Some, like Albert, keep giving over years and years." But he did more than give—another reason the staff lauded him when he came on his inspection visits—he raised money. During the time he was active in heading fund drives and solicitations from friends and acquaintances, La Rabida was close to self-sufficient, taking little from the University of Chicago in cash, though relying completely upon it for staff doctors and nurses.

Those who looked back on the crucial years of La Rabida's transformation from a small, private institution to an integral part of one of America's greatest universities, saw Albert in different ways. All of them agreed that, as Lowell Coggeshall put it, "it was Albert Pick, Jr., who was primarily responsible" for the affiliation. And all admired his forceful push once he took over the Board of Trustees; he had a goal that others had had, but he was the one to see it through to a conclusion. Where Albert "blurred" was when viewed by men and women separately. The women tended to see him as courteous, more nearly courtly, a gentleman, carefully and decorously dressed, polite and gentle. If occasionally there was a twinkle in his eye and a comment that might have been taken as suggestive by some, most were not aware of it, others ignored it, a few appreciated it. Grace Welsh, president and later lifetime member of the women's board, recalled him as a man who "liked women, who always made them feel important and capable," who had "high standards; he wouldn't take off his coat and tie at dinner," and who was firm and "businesslike" at board meetings, which he hosted for years at lunches at the Pick-Congress Hotel. He would, remembered Mrs. Welsh, "listen to others, encourage them by his example, inspire them to do more, to give as much as they could, and, as part of his position, when he was running the meetings, be all business."

Albert Dorfman, who returned full-time to the University of Chicago after his tenure at La Rabida had ended, recalled a man who, though he felt the hospital was "his," with all the warmth and personal attachment that implied for the children who were there and the small staff of thirty to forty close-knit people, still was careful not to interfere with the running of it. He left that to Dorfman and, in policy matters, did not attempt to override or alter full board decisions. His financial advisor, Siegmund Katz, acted as La Rabida's financial advisor as well and was brought to board meetings by Albert (and made a member of the board); but he did not question Katz's financial advice or measures Katz took as long as the board was kept informed and involved in the decisions.

Still, he did not, remembered Dorfman, run the board meetings with as firm a hand as he might have. He suffered from hypertension from the age of 50 on, and he tended on occasion to withdraw slightly from the discussion at hand. As a result, meetings often were "not sharp; his was not a tight, well-planned administration; he was not always well organized." Yet he was pleasant and amiable: "He was rarely sharp or contemptuous with people publicly," Dorfman said, "though he might bring something up years later and then talk contemptuously about the people who did whatever annoyed or disgusted him."

The impression left on most of those who knew Albert in those busy, productive years when, through La Rabida, he was finding a new kind of satisfaction, recall him as a man self-confident of his wealth and status, having achieved both on his own without any dependence of late on his father. This confidence and his feelings of protectiveness toward La Rabida were never more apparent than the day he escorted Prince Philip of England through the hospital. In Chicago, as part of a national visit to a number of cities, the Prince had heard of La Rabida before he got there. But his schedule was full, and he was surrounded by equerries. When one of the small children gave him a picture she had drawn for him, he absent-mindedly put it down and left it there when he left the room. The child burst into tears. Albert snatched up the picture and raced down the hall. 'Don't touch the prince!" someone shouted, but Albert caught up to him and held out the picture. "You left this behind, your highness," he said. "And the child who drew it for you is terribly unhappy."

The prince apologized and returned to the room. "I had forgotten this," he told the child, "and it was returned to me." He thanked her again, and he and Albert left, with the child now glowing with happiness. If Albert was impressed with the personal care of the staff at La Rabida, his own personal caring was as visible as their. And the visible expression of the way others felt about him was the sculpture commissioned by the employees of the Pick Hotel Corporation. The idea was initiated by Nadine Van Sant, Albert's long-time secretary: that Virginio Ferrari make a copy of the bust he had made of Albert to stand in the Pick's living room. The employees presented the bust to La Rabida to express their loyalty and pride in him.

11

Fifty Years and the University of Chicago

IT WAS a round number—fifty—a dignified and substantial number representing years and experience and dreams. He had graduated from the University of Chicago fifty years before, in 1977; he had married Corinne the same year. Now it was time to build, to establish concretely the ties that had been formed so long ago and had held steady over the years.

The strong ties had never weakened: Albert had never "left" the university. His long relationship with La Rabida kept him in touch with the men and women and departments of the institution he had first seen in University High School. On May 25, 1959, on the recommendation of the nominating comittee, headed by Gaylord Donnelley, Chicago printing and publishing magnate, he was elected to the Board of Trustees of the University of Chicago. He thus joined some of the city's leading businessmen, among them Walter Paepcke, John Nuveen, Gardner Stern, and Fairfax Cone. Many of the men on the board would become Albert's friends as well as coworkers in the running of the university.

He was an active member of the board, as aroused by the concerns of the university as he was by those of La Rabida and, in a different way, the many facets of his world of business. He became a member of the Budget Committee, the most powerful of the Board's working committees, which put him at the center of the university's life. He reveled in that, using his experience, his understanding of people, and his quick sense of the uses of money to formulate budgets and priorities and work with the people who then had to live with them.

It was said of him later that he formed relationships with people rather than with institutions. He would have agreed, gladly. He was generally impatient with institutions and their bureaucracies; he wanted done what he thought should be done and tried to brush past impediments where he found them. In one-to-one relationships, he often felt he was bypassing formulas and regulations. He knew, of course, that that was not always the case, and he knew when he was not successful at pushing an idea through to speedy conclusion; but, as a university professor later recalled, he was "terribly anxious to keep trying."

Much of Albert's relationship with the University of Chicago and two other universities—Northwestern near Chicago and Miami in Florida—was grounded in his dichotomous attitude toward people and money. Having wealth, he was accustomed to service, obedience, modern forms of obeisance and gratitude. At the same time, he was anxious to be loved and admired. With individuals, he was warm and outgoing, at times unassuming, with a wit that did not attack but still could pinpoint foibles. He expected much from others; he was willing to give as much himself. So his dealings with institutions swung from the "personal" in which he tried to mimic his interactions with individual men and women, to the formal, sometimes cold, sometimes angry, and often lofty behavior of the successful businessman and philanthropist dealing with academics. As might be expected, there was as much frustration as satisfaction in these arcs of interaction.

But in his work on the Board of Trustees he found mainly satisfaction. In addition to the Budget Committee, he served on the Committee on Business Administration and as co-chair-man for special gifts on the Policy Committee for Develop-ment. This last was of special interest; he was thinking more and more of significant ways to give to the university and at the same time perpetuate the Pick name that he traced through his father to his grandfather, uncle, and great grandfather.

As he looked about the university, he could name a number of areas in which he could give support. He had made some gifts to Billings, the teaching hospital of the University. He was founder and president of the Emeritus Club of the Alumni Association, a member of the Visiting Committee to the College, and a trustee member of the Council on Medical and Biological Research. And, perhaps most important of all of these, he was a member of the Board of Governors of In-ternational House and in that capacity had brought the house back from a position of weakness to one of strength.

International House was not a part of the university, but its Board of Governors was virtually identical in membership to the Board of Trustees of the University and, as a service, the University handled the budget and financial bookwork of the house. As its name made clear, the International House was home to a varied group of students from as many nations as were represented in the university's student body at any time. Of the same Gothic architecture as the rest of the campus, venerable gray stone cooled by ivy, the building stood square and solidly reassuring at the corner of 59th and Blackstone Streets, on the periphery of the campus but still on the edge of the sweeping panorama of green—the Midway Plaisance—that bisects the campus east to west.

The building (and three others with the same name and function in Paris, New York, and Berkeley, California) had been constructed with money from John D. Rockefeller (when another Rockefeller gift was made—the awesome Rockefeller Chapel a few blocks west of International House—students went about the campus chanting, "John D., from whom oil blessings flow."); and it was Rockefeller money that provided rooms rent-free to students and kept the house alive through each year's deficit. Finally, the Board of Governors, under its president, Pete Russell, president of the Harris Trust and Savings Bank and a friend from Albert's Blackfriar's days at the University, turned to Albert as one who had some experience in the housing of temporary guests and asked him to look at the stubborn problems of the house.

He was delighted. It was as if he had been preparing for the moment when experience would join with emotion—his strong desire to take hold and physically help "his" university. He brought in some of his best people from the Albert Pick Hotels and gave them the assignment of conducting studies of the operation of the house and its financial standing.

They clocked the work of the maids, and found they were cleaning four rooms a day; at Albert Pick Hotels, a maid cleaned sixteen rooms a day. They interviewed Mrs. Goodspeed, who supervised the maids, and Mr. Fultz, who had managed the house since hired by the Rockefeller family. They checked invoices and dusty ledgers, they walked through the halls and the more than 500 rooms and poked into corners and closets, and beneath stairs.

In the end, they fired the old guard and hired a new group to run the house like a hotel, using business methods the Pick Hotels used successfully in city after city, though circumstances and guest populations differed. Within a year, the deficit began to drop; it went from $75,000 to $32,000; and in two more years, to zero. David Rockefeller wrote to the Board of Governors of International House asking why no requests had come for checks to make up the annual deficits. The board, as gleeful as children who have just learned to walk, replied, "We have Albert Pick to advise us."

Albert talked about International House in later years with a personal pride he could not muster for the hotel chain. He recalled the house's "100% occupancy with no debt" that "no hotel could achieve." He remembered the phrase with which the board had replied to David Rockefeller, and Rockefeller's subsequent request that Albert travel to the other Rockefeller International Houses, in New York, Berkeley, and Paris, to reorganize them. And he recalled, a bit wryly, the letter he wrote refusing the request. He had, he said, quite enough to do running one business. But he would be glad to give David Rockefeller his "secrets." And, in a lengthy memo, he detailed the management techniques and cost-saving measures he had used to pull International House to a level of solvency, for the edification of a Rockefeller.

Perhaps the major reason for the keen pleasure he received from the successful reorganization of International House was its connection with the University of Chicago. As the years saw the solid establishment of his hotel chain as one of the country's largest, his attention was more and more focusing on subjects that, in the long run, would give him the most enduring satisfaction. These tended to revolve around the young. La Rabida was the institution most directly involved with the care and nurturing of the young; and his deep love for the hospital was a result of the opportunity it gave him to form close, almost intimate, relationships with the men and women who "did for" children and the children who lived there.

In a larger way, he did the same at institutions of higher learning. He saw students in a special glow: the future of the country, the future of families and families of nations. And so he looked to universities as the hope, perhaps the only hope, for peace and justice. He would know a number of politicians in his time, and leaders that included two Presidents, but his faith was to remain in the power of education rather than with the powerful few.

His interests and his emotions came together in 1967, the fiftieth anniversary of his marriage to Corinne. He wanted to build a theater in her honor, in her name; and he wanted it to be a part of the University of Chicago. There had been talk for some time of an arts complex at the university, ambitious by itself, but even more so as part of the "Campaign for Chicago" launched in 1965 to raise 160 million dollars for growth and development of the university.

The university had received a one-million-dollar Ford Foundation grant, not restricted to any one project but available for the arts complex. Albert proposed the Corinne Frada Pick Theater and plunged into the project in correspondence with university officials, lawyers, trustees, and professors. On December 28, 1967, he wrote to the directors and officers of the Albert Pick, Jr., Fund:

> I have pledged to the University of Chicago the face amount of $1,500,000 in municipal bonds which . . . are to be given to the University subject to a life income from them on Corinne's and my part, but after the death of both of us they are to be the property of the University of Chicago. In consideration of this gift the University of Chicago is to build on its campus a theater of approximately 600 seats to be known as the "Corinne Frada Pick Theater."

By July, 1968, the trust agreement had been drawn up by Albert's lawyer, Alan Altheimer; in August, the university had responded; and by December 9, 1968, the final agreement, irrevocable and non-amendable, was signed. Albert immediately turned his attention to the choice of an architect, receiving suggestions from a number of sources, including William Benton, publisher of the Encyclopaedia Britannica, who strongly urged the selection of the Frank Lloyd Wright Associates of Taliesen West.

It was a heady time, with talk of architectural designs for "the gem of the campus," as President Edward Levi called it, major stories in all of Chicago's newspapers, gratitude and congratulations from university faculty and staff and many alumni as well, and the emotional thrust of working with the university and building for Corinne at the same time.

But the heady time was relatively brief; the months dragged, with nothing visible taking place. Questioning, complaining, impatient letters came from Albert's office; but no money was spent by the university. It appeared that the Ford grant had been used for other purposes. At some point in the long trail of correspondence and discussions, Albert began to feel the project would never be completed, that they had reached or were past the point of repairing what seemed to be serious damage to his gift, to the spirit in which he made it, and to the cordiality, even, as he thought, affection, which he and the university officials had shared.

Strangely, at the same time, another project which would bear the Pick name was moving ahead smoothly, on schedule. In 1967, as a member of the Board of Trustees of the university, Albert learned of a grant from the Ford Foundation of 8.5 million dollars for International Studies, of which one million was for a building. He became enormously excited about the project—a perfect chance to combine his interests in young people and in international relations. (That same year, he was asked by Dwight Eisenhower to serve as a director of the People-to-People movement which Eisenhower had founded.)

The building not only had the Ford Foundation behind it; a $700,000 grant also had come from the National Science Foundation. All that was needed, according to the university, to complete the building envisioned by Chauncy Harris, Dean of the School of International Studies, was $750,000.

Albert pledged the funds and became as deeply immersed in plans for this new building as he was in plans for the theater. Still, he kept the projects separate in his mind. Letters to university officials dealt with one building or the other, though the same official might get two letters on the same day or in the same week. To President Edward Levi, with whom Albert was becoming disenchanted over the lagging theater program, went a warm letter on April 29, 1969, as he and Corinne were leaving for Europe, saying that, when they returned in June, he wanted to talk about the building for International Studies. No mention was made of the theater.

In the same way, Michael Claffey, Vice-President for Development, wrote Albert on June 9, 1969, reporting on the groundbreaking for the International Studies Building on the previous May 19 and asking when he and Corinne would like to make a site visit on their return from Europe. No mention was made of the theater building, though other letters from Claffey dealt with it at great length.

Letters flew back and forth between Florida, where Albert and Corinne went after their European trip, and Chicago, and between Albert's office in Chicago and offices on the campus of the University of Chicago. Albert approved the plans of Ralph Rapson, dean of the school of architecture at the University of Minnesota and architect of the Guthrie Theater in Minneapolis, which Albert had admired, and the U.S. Embassy office buildings in Stockholm and Copenhagen. At first, he had thought the building "too modern"; but later, he was a strong advocate of the clean bold lines Rapson favored.

He made it a condition of his gift that a sculpture be placed in front of the building, the commission to go to his young protege, Virginio Ferrari. Albert and Corinne had met Ferrari on one of their trips to Italy; the sweeping lines, earth-bound but leaping and stretching outward, of Ferrari's cast sculptures excited both of them; and the young artist, with his beautiful wife and son, instilled in them strong protective feelings. Ferrari's youth and lack of renown even in his native Italy, together with what Albert and Corinne saw as a brilliant talent, encouraged their protectiveness; but it surely was enhanced by Albert's desire to bring the arts into his philanthropies. Music, theater, sculpture—he wanted all to be part of the world he gave as well as the world he enjoyed. So he and Corinne virtually "adopted" the Ferraris. In letters and in person, the young couple called them Papa Pick and Mama Pick, and when the Ferraris came to America, Albert and Corinne rented them an apartment on the south side of Chicago near the University of Chicago, whose faculty Ferrari had joined. And as Albert was looking for commissions for Ferrari, what better place than in buildings he was giving as gifts?

The sculpture for the International Relations Building was not formally decided upon until August, 1970, when Ferrari was given the commission; that same week, he left for Italy to work in the bronze foundry with which he was familiar. The sculpture was to be in place by the beginning of the fall quarter at the university.

But well before that date, talks on the sculpture and the sculptor had been underway; they never were far from Albert's mind. So close to the surface were they that, as Albert later recalled, when an unrelated event came up—his negotiations with Chicago merchandiser Sol Polk over some land Albert was selling and Polk was buying —Albert turned it to the advantage of the University.

The land was north of Chicago in a semi-rural area where Albert's father at one time had owned a great deal of property and Albert himself had bought extensively. In their negotiations, Albert and Polk were within $25,000 of the price one wanted to pay and the other wanted to receive. Finally, Albert said, "We're both stubborn men, and neither of us is going to budge. So let this settle it: the difference between us will go to philanthropy."

So Sol Polk's check for $25,000 went to the University of Chicago, for the theater, as Albert requested. A short time later, Albert asked for, and received, Polk's permission to transfer the funds to help pay for Ferrari's sculpture. He himself added $5,000 to make the total. As Chauncy Harris later recalled, "The Polks had not the slightest interest in the University of Chicago or in a sculpture, but Albert got the money to go there, which was a good example of the way he made things happen."

He could make many things happen; when he could not,

when he was stymied, he was doubly frustrated, for he found it very difficult to respond with anger. It may have been the memory of his father roaring through the house with explosions of temper that terrified the four children and sent Gertrude to her room; it may have been, in part, his own calmer temperament or ability to repress anger. The result was that, though he may have felt anger and frustration, he internalized them; and, in conversation and correspondence, he often flailed like a boy new to roller skates, trying one tentative maneuver after another but in the long run not getting very far.

So it was with the theater at the University of Chicago: he pushed and pulled and moved to one side and another with various university administrators, but no progress was made. Later, he would say the University "dragged its feet for three years." In fact, he knew the university was trying to raise funds to build the theater and a number of other structures, and that it was doing so in the 1960s and early 1970s when student demonstrations against American military policies and specifically the war in Vietnam on campuses throughout the country, the University of Chicago not excepted, were occupying the attention of university administrators and creating caution in past and potential donors.

The university had its hands full. (Albert knew that, too: he wrote to Vice-President Charles Daly, sympathizing with the university in its "difficult times" and saying he thought the administration was doing a good job in handling them.) The original impetus from the theater building had been positive and filled with good will, even to the extent of preparing a magnificent oversize book, printed on heavy parchment with watercolor illustrations from the great dramas of the world, to be used in raising funds for the Corinne Frada Pick Theater. But the Ford Foundation funds had gone to meet more immediate needs in the brief hiatus of giving that occurred in those disturbed times, and new money which had been anticipated had not come in.

It was not stated whether or not Albert was asked to give cash, as he had done with the International Studies Building, even if only enough to get the theater started. In any event, the thought must have occurred to him more than once, since it was lack of immediate funds that was holding the project up. But he held firm and refused to do more than he had done with the 1.5 million dollars in municipal bonds available to the University only on his and Corinne's death.

Finally, Edward Levi suggested a smaller theater than the various ones which had been discussed (the latest proposal had been for two theaters in one building, one of 100 seats and the other of 250, in the round). The new proposal was for a theater of fewer than 500 seats. Albert rejected it out-of-hand as too small and, feeling betrayed, wrote a memo detailing all the actions on the theater from the time of his first offer to April 21, 1970, when Corinne suggested that he "get out of" the contract with the university.

Fairfax Cone, head of one of Chicago's most successful advertising agencies and a member of the Board of Trustees, and Lawrence Kimpton, former chancellor of the university and close friend of Albert's, stepped in to effect a compromise. Through the spring of 1970, they worked on amending and revoking the non-amendable and irrevocable agreement Albert and the university had signed.

On May 21, 1970, Albert wrote to Fairfax Cone, stating that "the smaller theater proposed by President Levi is not acceptable to Mrs. Pick and me, and I do not wish my contribution to the university to be used for its construction."

He went on to describe a suggestion he, Cone, and Kimpton had discussed at a luncheon the previous week for the immediate gift of $200,000 if matched by the university through its Women's Board or Board of Trustees, to the rehabilitation of Midway Studios for art and sculpture (where Ferrari was sculptor-in-residence). He offered, as well, $900,000 toward a Corinne F. Pick Theater of 1,000 seats designed and built by the Taliesen Associated Architects of the Frank Lloyd Wright Foundation if and when the university found the 1.6 million dollars to go ahead with the structure. The offer was good for three years only.

He was still flailing, reluctant to commit himself for anything like the sums necessary for the theater, and the question arises whether his commitment to the theater was as great as he claimed. Corinne preferred a concert hall at Northwestern University in Evanston, where she had studied music shortly after she and Albert were married; and, though she had encouraged Albert in his gifts to the University of Chicago, her own reluctance (which did not develop until well after the glow of the initial gift announcement) may have influenced Albert to play with figures instead of concrete realizable plans. In any event, his gift became hedged with so many restrictions and delays of his own (even spilling over to the International Studies Building where his $750,000 gift promised for 1967 was not made until October 7, 1970) that there could be little but increased frustration and tensions over the theater.

In the end, as suggested by Edward Levi, and with a measure of amicability that could survive because of the International Studies Building simultaneously taking shape as a foil to the distress of the theater project, 1.2 million dollars of the municipal bonds would be subject to appointment in Albert's will, with $300,000 going to the University of Chicago on the death of the survivor of Albert and Corinne. The theater dream at Albert's school was ended; soon, one at Corinne's would begin.

But in the meantime strained relations were being mended. Albert and Levi had had an angry telephone conversation on the size of the theater as each recalled it in its various incarnations. Levi's brief letter of apology for the "misunderstanding" over the size of the theater arrived the next day; the two men had lunch a few hours later and talked of the International Studies Building and other issues involving the university as a whole.

In the months that followed, as Ferrari's sculpture was commissioned and the building built, they kept in cool but regular touch. And on October 12, 1970, Levi wrote to Albert a finely hyperbolic letter that truly closed the book on the theater project and the emotions it aroused:

Dear Albert,
These are difficult times for the University and, I guess, for many of us. Frequently it is the gift which comes in difficult times which has the most meaning, and makes the greatest difference. That is certainly true here.
The field of International Studies has never been more important. The kinds of contribution which scholars from this University over time can make in this area are many, and are related to a variety of disciplines. The Albert Pick Hall for International Studies will most surely be one of the most significant buildings on the campus. As you know, in many of the area study fields, the University of Chicago has been regarded as having scholars among the strongest in our country. This could not possibly last unless we could house them properly, nor could their work proceed without adequate offices and seminar rooms. And this is what the Albert Pick Hall for International Studies will provide. The Albert Pick Hall will make all the difference in the world to the University. I think it will make considerable difference to the world.
And so I want you to know, representing this University and its scholars, and speaking very much for myself also— how grateful I am to you.

At Thanksgiving of that year, another letter from Levi said simply, "Dear Albert: The building is becoming more beautiful every day. It is really taking shape."

And the waters, to a great extent, were smoothed.

◊

The Albert Pick Hall for International Studies has become a focus of interest among other important architectural statements on the University of Chicago campus (created by luminaries including Mies Van der Rohe, Eero Saarinen, Perkins and Will and Skidmore, Owings & Merrill). Ralph Rapson used huge slabs of limestone and vertical columns to blend with the Gothic tone of the campus buildings, but there is a strong sense of modernity, expressed in Rapson's devotion to assymetry, banks of dark-tinted windows and overhanging upper floors that break up traditional "corners" of the building and create a sense of flowing cohesion.

The bronze Ferrari sculpture, "Dialogo" (Dialogue), looms in front on a limestone base, three of its elements soaring upward and coming together at the top in a show of strength and community, the fourth resting low but pointing toward the uniting of the other three like a wave rushing upon the shore.

At the dedication ceremony on June 14, 1971, Harold Hayden, Professor of Art at the University, concluded his remarks with:

> The quiet strength and gesture of Dialogo achieving unity in diversity give expression to ideals to which the Albert Pick Hall is dedicated, the coming together of men and nations in peaceful communication.

Like the other speeches, Hayden's was brief and warm. Levi, less hyperbolic than in his letter to Albert, said:

> It is a long chance to say that justice and international order will be measurably increased by what is done here. It is a long chance that the ideas and understanding will help remove the self-inflicted pain of mankind that "boys are only born to be buried beneath tall grass." Yet all this is possible, and no search can have a greater value.

The ceremony opened with Chauncy Harris, Samuel N. Harper Professor in the Department of Geography and Director of the Center for International Studies at the University. Of all the speakers, he seemed the most moved by the day, by the promise of the building. He paid homage to the "remarkable cooperation" among "three different types of donors" to the building: "a philanthropic foundation, a government foundation, and a private donor," saying such cooperation "augurs well for the aspiration of the programs carried on in this build-ing to encourage such cooperation on an international scale." He spoke of the possibilities of international studies for pre-venting wars or major international conflicts or flights of refu-gees and in improving the economic and social lot of groups of the world's citizens. And then he summed up by describing the view from the Albert Pick Hall of the campus in all directions. He concluded:

> It is my hope that the Albert Pick Hall for International Studies will not only open vistas of the immediate physical campus . . . but will enlarge the vision and imagination of students and faculty to the great world beyond the cam-pus, both Western and non-Western, developed and develop-ing, and that in this enlarged arena, this building will con-tribute to the understanding and appreciation which peoples of the world have for one another and thus in some small measure contribute to a richer life for all and a more just and peaceful world.

Albert stood to speak as Harris's words died away. He had a strong feeling of history, a sense that this occasion, this gift, the future they symbolized, had allowed him to participate in something new in his life. As long as he lived, this sense of historic vitality would stay with him, and his achievements in the business world would pale beside it. He spoke of his roots in the city and the University of Chicago, his family going back 126 years, and he himself entering University High School sixty-two years earlier. He recalled his meetings with then President Dwight Eisenhower, who had spoken broodingly and bitterly of the horrors and futility of war. And then he spoke personally:

> In contributing toward the Albert Pick Hall, I feel that I have done something to honor my predecessors, my family, my grandfather, and his oldest brother, the original Albert Pick. I would like to express the hope that this building will contribute to international understanding and world peace.

Pauline Ross, Albert and Corinne's granddaughter, daughter of their daughter Gladys, unveiled the Ferrari sculpture and a reception followed. Albert later remembered the day as an enormously satisfying one, not least because of a letter he received a week after the ceremony from Edward Levi, which said in part:

> I am particularly delighted that the new building carries your name. You have been a staunch citizen of the University—as student, alumnus, and Trustee—and you have helped the University overcome obstacles and take advantage of new responsibilities and opportunities in many areas. . . .
>
> Plans, as we know, sometimes go wrong, and good deeds do not result in the deep satisfaction and pleasure which should be expected. My hope is that this beautiful new building and the work which will go on in it, and the strength which it will give to the entire University, will give to Corinne and to you the pleasure and satisfaction which we all share.

He could not have asked for a more fitting conclusion to his building program at the University of Chicago.

12

Universities
North and South

IN THE decade from 1967 to 1977, Albert made his greatest
commitment to the strengthening of educational institutions. His trust in education as a force for progress never
wavered; equally staunch was his faith in the men and women
who taught in those institutions—and in the students, as well.
At no time in the history of his philanthropy did he attempt to
influence the content or direction of studies in the buildings
that bore the Pick name, nor the events scheduled in them.
It was a strangely diffident attitude that contrasted with the
instinctively authoritative attitude of other times. Yet, he always
made the distinction between the activities that made possible
a physical structure, whatever that structure symbolized, and
the activities that went on within its walls when it was complete. His job, important as he saw it, was finished when the
financing was accomplished and the small, sometimes insigni-
ficant, supervisory authority he was granted by grateful university administrators had come to an end with the last coat of
paint and the last tree tamped in place.

But buildings were in fact a small part of his educational
philanthropy. In schools from one end of the country to the
other, scholarships bear his or Corinne's name: Rollins College,

Florida; Roosevelt University in Chicago; Berea of Kentucky; Cornell University; Florida State University; Michigan State University; Oklahoma State University; Pennsylvania State University; the University of Denver; the University of Houston; the City College of San Francisco; the Michigan Colleges Foundation; the Olio Foundation of Independent Colleges; and the United Negro College Fund; all received gifts, many on an annual basis, and scholarships. Wherever he heard of a need, or a program that gave promise of future rewards in research and scholarship, he reached for his pen. Each time, he felt he was giving to anonymous but individual students and individual programs in otherwise large and impersonal institutions; he did his best to enhance the personal, individual sphere.

Yet, inevitably, he would relate and give to institutions, though he would attempt over and over again to personalize the procedures as he did at La Rabida Sanitorium, where he could describe the rooms and equipment used by specific nurses and doctors whose names and faces he knew. And he knew, too, at least by sight, many of the children who spent weeks, months, sometimes years there in beds he endowed, in a library with his brother Laurence's portrait in it, in the Gertrude Frank Pick Children's Center named for his mother.

In a sense, it was a personal "introduction" that led him to the University of Miami; his father had preceded him there, donating money for the School of Music Library (which bears Albert, Sr.'s name) and receiving an honorary degree shortly before he died. In addition, Albert and Corinne had become close friends of Henry King Stanford, president of the University, and his wife Ruth, as well as some of the faculty members.

In the same way, Albert and Corinne were friendly with Roscoe Miller, president of Northwestern University in Evanston, Illinois. Perhaps more important, Corinne had studied music there after they were married; she felt it was as much "her" school as the University of Chicago was Albert's.

And so, when Albert began to think in philanthropic terms

larger than monetary gifts and scholarships, he had three Universities interwoven with his and Corinne's life; and it was to them that he turned.

During the time he was negotiating with the University of Chicago for a theater building and a school of international studies, he also was being courted by the other two schools. Northwestern's staff and faculty approached him in 1970 to tell him of their ambitious plans to expand the campus by building on landfill into Lake Michigan (the campus, squeezed along the lake shore by the city of Evanston had nowhere to go but into the water). The new campus, to be named for the university's president and Albert's friend, J. Roscoe Miller, was to hold, among other buildings, a Fine and Performing Arts Center, including the School of Music. Albert expressed to Dean George Howerton, who sent him the information, specific interest in that proposed project.

In correspondence that followed, Albert was kept informed of every step the university took. In a letter of December 2, 1970, Franklin Kreml, Vice-President for Planning and Development, wrote him that the architects for Northwestern's future Music Center were to meet with university planners and Jonathan Edwards of the Chicago Symphony Orchestra to travel to Champaign, Illinois, to study the University of Illinois Krannert Music Center, called one of the finest acoustic halls in the country (the Chicago Symphony Orchestra made many of its recordings there).

Barely three weeks later, Albert and Corinne met with the architect (Edward Dart of Loebl, Schlossman, Bennett and Dart), John Wilson, Northwestern's planning coordinator, and Kreml to discuss financing the Corinne Frada Pick Concert Hall of the School of Music of Northwestern University. And on December 29, a few days later, Kreml sent a letter detailing the discussion of the meeting, a discussion filled with contingencies and brave hopes.

Northwestern's plans—as all University plans—were ambitious. The estimated cost of the Performing Arts Center was approximately 14 million dollars (in 1970), of which 2.5 million dollars had been allocated to the Concert Recital Hall. But the university wanted to combine in one structure the Concert Hall and the School of Music, to reduce costs. Their estimates indicated the savings would be from forty to seventy-five percent. The cost of the music school was pegged at 8.5 million dollars.

At the time, university officials had been holding a series of meetings with Chicago philanthropist Helen Regenstein, widow of Joseph Regenstein, who had built his printing company to one of the largest in the country. Mrs. Regenstein, through the family foundation, would give millions to the University of Chicago for its new library and more millions in the field of medicine. Northwestern thought she would give eight to ten million dollars for the Performing Arts Center, but they were not sure. Albert's gift of two-and-a-half million, if he made it, would have to await Mrs. Regenstein's, if she made it, to be used to build the combined School of Music and the Concert Hall.

Kreml included in his letter mention of the trust established at the University of Chicago for the Theater Building (he thought it was revocable) and suggested that Albert change it to an irrevocable one to pay Northwestern two million dollars on the death of the survivor of Corinne and himself.

The situation was not far from the one that had prevailed at the University of Chicago not so many years before. Albert still was trying to present the 50th anniversary gift he had promised Corinne; if it could not be at the University of Chicago, it could be at Northwestern with equal appropriateness. He was no more ready than before to make a cash gift to the University; but he was willing to see what his attorney Alan Altheimer, could work out with Northwestern's attorneys so that, assuming Helen Regenstein made her gift, he could use the funds in the trust at the University of Chicago to build a concert hall for Corinne in Evanston. (Later, when negotiations at Northwestern were more advanced, he would say, in pushing for yet more speed on the building of the Recital Hall, that he was not getting any younger and he wanted "to escort my bride down the aisle of her theater." For a time that became his greatest urgency.)

As it happened, Helen Regenstein and her son Joseph, Jr., said the foundation had to rebuild its funds after the drain on them for the University of Chicago Regenstein Library, and they asked if "Mr. Pick couldn't wait a year" to see the entire Arts complex begun. By then, Albert and Altheimer had worked out the agreement to transfer four-fifths of the one-and-a-half million in trust at the University of Chicago to Northwestern, leaving Northwestern 1.2 million dollars on the death of him and Corinne, plus another $800,000 from Albert's estate on his death alone. The agreement was accompanied by a carefully drafted and edited letter from Albert to Roscoe Miller, detailing the name, site, and architects of the Corinne Frada Pick Concert Hall, reviewing his disappointment at "the lethargic attitude" of the University of Chicago, and concluding:

> I sincerely trust that Corinne's and my hopes and expectations in this matter will be realized and that we will not have any cause for complaint about dilatory tactics, but quite the contrary will be thrilled with the dispatch with which this entire project will be handled.

That sentence was changed in the final version (Altheimer had written in the margin of the draft, "a little strong") to read:

> I sincerely trust that Corinne's and my hopes and expectations in this matter will be realized and that both we and the officers and trustees of Northwestern University will have every reason to be pleased and gratified."

His impatience was visible; but he knew that, as long as he was not offering cash for immediate building, he was as dependent upon other events as was the University. In this case, he and the university officials were waiting for the Regensteins; and when the Regensteins said the money could not be committed for at least a year, proceedings had to come to a halt. Albert responded to Franklin Kreml on June 17, 1971, that he was disappointed with (and implied he could not understand) the refusal of Helen Regenstein even to write a letter of intent to make a major gift in the next year or two or three, with which the university "could then proceed immediately on the final plans and even on the building using their pledge and mine as collateral for such financing as would be necessary. . . ." He closed that letter with:

> In the meantime I continue to get pressure from other universities, and while assuredly my first choice is to go through with my intention of financing a recital hall in honor of my wife, I feel very uncomfortable being in limbo, so to speak.

On December 3, he reiterated to Roscoe Miller his desire to build at Northwestern instead of somewhere else, and added:

> Rocky, assuming that this will be done, it will cement a long friendship between you and me, enhance Corinne's and my interest in Northwestern which has existed for many years, and perhaps encourage us to go a little further particularly if conditions are favorable financially for us which I trust they will be.

But neither implied threats, promises, nor cajoling helped. A week later, on December 10, Miller replied:

> . . . it is purely a question of money. We cannot at this time see our way clear to go ahead with the project.
>
> This does not mean we have not been trying, and we will continue to try. However, in all fairness I must point out that you do not have an obligation here and, if you wish to make other arrangements, I can see why you might want to do so. . . . You have no idea how it pains me to have to write this letter.

Northwestern dedicated three new buildings in 1972 as part of a 180-million-dollar development program: the Norris University Center (student union) with funds from the general pool of contributions to the fund drive; the Nathanial Leverone Graduate School of Management, funded by Mrs. Leverone in memory of her husband; and the School of Education's Center for the Teaching Professions, funded by the W. K. Kellogg Foundation. Roscoe Miller certainly would have liked to add, in the announcements of those three buildings, the commitment for an arts complex on the landfill east of the campus (an area to bear his name); the fact that he could not do so was vivid evidence that the university could not find the money, nor raise enough of the 16 million dollars on Albert's trust of 1.2 million dollars to go ahead.

The project was revived from an unexpected source. Charles Staiger, who had been married to Albert's sister Pauline for less than a year when she died in 1931, wrote to Albert that he was seeking a way to commemorate her and find a home for his collection of Oriental art at the the same time. He had bought the pieces in his travels for Harry Winston jewelers and had held them ever since. Now his second wife, of thirty-five years, was dying; and she agreed with him that the best thing to do with them was to donate them to an institution and, in fact, perhaps even build an art gallery to house them that would bear Pauline's name.

Discussion with Northwestern was begun again, in February, 1972, on the basis of a one-thousand-seat recital hall with an art gallery attached, or as a separate but connected building. The building, according to both Staiger and Albert, was to be a "gem" on the Northwestern campus; Albert seemed to have put out of his mind for good the "gem of the campus" that the theater at the University of Chicago was to have been.

Staiger came to Florida in March; lawyers, architects, university officials, and Albert met in June in Chicago to draft a plan for proceeding. By then the university had abandoned its plans for a sixteen-million-dollar complex; the Board of Trustees had authorized the borrowing of three million dollars for a concert hall and adjoining art gallery. The original plans had to be scrapped, since it was impossible to scale them down to a three-million-dollar building; and while the architects set out to design a new building, Staiger and his attorneys worked with Northwestern's attorneys on two gifts: money for building, and art objects for the gallery.

Albert had been through it before. He knew the proceedings would have their own rhythm, and there was little anyone could do to speed them up. He tried, as always, by pushing for action in paragraphs of his letters; but the months went by, and even Staiger, he felt, was not doing all he could to help. He wrote a Christmas greeting on December 22, 1972, explaining a little impatiently the tax advantages ("a large tax deduction which has a carryover for five years. . . .") if Staiger acted soon. Jack Fields, of Northwestern's Development Department, arranged for an appraisal of Staiger's Oriental art collection and his real estate in Massachusetts in January of 1973, and that seemed to break the last barrier. Funds and art objects were brought together in legal documents; and six months later, in July, 1973, Albert was describing arrangements for a luncheon/groundbreaking ceremony in a letter to Staiger. Albert was in high spirits: a man who had waited a long time and suddenly saw the strands of dozens of letters, conversations, memos, and delayed hopes come together in what seemed to be a resolution that was also a physical structure. (Corinne, too, saw it as a culmination of hopes and dreams; at the dedication ceremony, she would call the Concert Hall her "shining palace built upon the sands" beside Lake Michigan.)

Albert, Corinne, and Staiger wielded silver-sprayed picks to break ground for the Pick-Staiger Concert Hall and Foyer-Gallery on July 25, 1973. The picks stand in front of the fireplace in the den of their Highland Park home, a symbol not only of a ceremony but of the gift Albert finally was able to give "his bride" for their 50th wedding anniversary.

The Pick-Staiger Concert Hall, designed by Edward Dart, is an elegant structure, architecturally and acoustically. Wide expanses of glass across the front of the precast concrete building lighten its mass, as does the glass wall between the lobby and the concert hall. Open stairways leading to the upper level and a walkway above the stage add to the sense of openness; at the same time, the acoustics create a feeling of intimacy with brilliant sound and resonance and response. The building has been cited for acoustic excellence; and, visually, it has become a focal point of the campus. Another focal point is the sculpture in front of the hall, which Albert had arranged for as early as 1971: Virginio Ferrari's "Armonia" (Harmony) which Albert and Corinne had first seen in Italy and which was purchased for the building.

The dedicatory concert was held October 26, 1975. Albert and Staiger spoke; and Corinne presented the key to the concert hall to James May, recipient that year of the Corinne Frada Pick scholarship in the school of music. The response was made by Thomas Miller, Dean of the School of Music. Presiding over the ceremony was the new president of the university, Robert Strotz, who thanked Albert and Corinne and Staiger for "this magnificent concert hall which will endure and touch us all."

That last phrase could not but please Albert and Corinne the most. The dedicatory concert featured the young pianist Ralph Votapek, who had won first prize in the International Van Cliburn Competition of 1962; but perhaps more significant to Albert and Corinne, while a student at Northwestern, Votapek had been the first student to hold the Corinne Frada Pick music scholarship. Albert and Corinne always would feel close to Votapek, who touched the audience with his performance of the Rachmaninoff Third Piano Concerto (the program, with Bernard Rubenstein conducting the University Symphony Orchestra, opened with Stravinsky's "Fanfare for a New Theater"), as they felt close to the individuals who performed and made up the audience in "their" hall. As with all their projects, they saw it as a conglomerate of individuals touching each other's lives, rather than as an institution with simply one more building. The idea of a hall that would "endure and touch us all" could not have expressed their own dreams more completely, and they both felt content.

〇

For a period of time, Albert was involved in simultaneous negotiations on three campuses. His interests, springing from different sources, were equal in all three: the University of Chicago as "his" school; Northwestern's as Corinne's; and the University of Miami as, in a roundabout way, his father's.

Albert, Sr., putting Chicago behind him and beginning to pull himself up from the well of his bankruptcy and his anger at dependence upon his son, determined to make himself a part of Miami as once he had been part of Chicago. With money left in his wife's trust and funds from Albert, Jr., plus a small but steady income from the two hotels he still considered "his own" (and Albert encouraged that), he began to buy real estate in and around what was then, in the early 1930s, the city limits of Miami. He and Albert, Jr., were, on the surface, cordial, even solicitous; but never again would they have even the brief moments of closeness they once had had, and while Albert's respect for his father had not wavered, his father's earlier treatment of him as—in Albert's words— "half a man" was not revived. Albert, Sr., treated his son as a successful businessman in a world of successful businessmen; he never credited him with any special acumen or other qualities in which fathers usually seek to take pride in their offspring.

But the two did buy land together, most notably parcels on

the Kane Concourse, and land where the Americana Hotel now stands, and Albert, Sr., bought other parcels and invested in a bank with Shepherd Broad, whose name appears on a number of Miami landmarks today. Within a few years—no time at all to those who measured aggressivity and success in terms of youth—Albert, Sr., had regained the life-style he had known in Chicago (and been known for): he was again "a plunger," as those in Chicago remembered him; and he was again juggling and manipulating in fine fettle. In short, he was once more a millionaire.

But to be a millionaire in Miami as he had been a millionaire in Chicago meant establishing himself as a part of the community—known, recognized, sought out as a leader. He turned to the academic world for this: a visible symbol in the community of the immediate use of wealth for legitimate, long-term purposes. And the academic world in Miami was its university, then small (in fact, little more than one building) and only beginning to have the plans that would come to fruition forty years later and bring the school some measure of renown.

Because of his wife's love of music, Albert, Sr., focused on the School of Music, funding its library and setting up some scholarships. The university honors those who give $50,000 or more as its "Founders"—Albert, Sr., became one of the "Founders" as his son would later. And the university also awarded Albert, Sr., an honorary doctorate in acknowledgement of his contributions to education, as later it would honor his son.

It was indeed in his father's footsteps that Albert walked in Miami. Because of his father, he felt the university there was as much "his" as those in Chicago and Evanston: part of the family. Then, too, on their regular winter sojourns in Miami, Albert and Corinne had become a part of the city and its social life and had met a number of university faculty members, including Jesse Spirer, who would become a lifelong friend, and

Henry King Stanford, president of the university, who would be Albert's close "contact" in his gifts to the institution, especially the international studies building.

Had he not been negotiating for several gifts at once, the process might have seemed wearisome and even, at times, fruitless. But since the activities overlapped, the fact that many of his letters to three different universities might have been interchanged with little noticeable disruption seems not to have struck him. Or perhaps he knew enough of institutions by then to understand the rituals in dealing with them and to go through the motions with less upheaval than otherwise.

That last is doubtful, however. He never wavered from his insistence on dealing with and responding to individuals, and he never lost his sense of frustration at obstacles in his way, no matter whether they sprang from bureaucracies, external events, or the foibles of individuals. So he went through motions, followed the requirements of ritual in dealing with institutions, and eventually accomplished most of what he set out to do—but he always would think it could have been done more easily and more harmoniously all along the line if he could just have sat down (of course with his lawyer) and come to simple agreements across friendly tables.

The first proposal to Albert from the University of Miami, through Stanford, was made in July, 1968, for a Center for Advanced International Studies. A formal, well-planned, thoughtful booklet of some seventy pages, it is impressive—and expensive: 3.3 million dollars was asked for construction and a curriculum program in Sino-Soviet studies.

Between that proposal in 1968 and 1974, when a final project was agreed upon, both the university and Albert made several proposals for varying amounts of money to be accumulated and used in varying ways. There was little pressure; the correspondence was leisurely, between gentlemen, with no sense of urgency. Yet the university, as all universties in the early 1970s, after the disruptions and uncertainties of the

1960s, needed funding; and all were in the midst of formulating or carrying out ambitious drives. There is probably no question that Albert enjoyed being "courted" during this time; in fact, his dismay at the University of Chicago may well have rested, at least in part, on the fact that Levi and the others did not court him but let his project lapse when he could not make the funds more of a reality in the immediate present. Whatever the reason, he received much more satisfaction from Northwestern and Miami in these years and took more pleasure from the buildings he gave to those institutions than to the Pick Center at the University of Chicago.

In 1973, Albert commissioned Virginio Ferrari to sculpt a bust of Henry King Stanford. It was both an expression of his desire to help Ferrari when he could and also of his affection for Stanford. At the same time, Albert made arrangements for Ferrari to do another bust, this time of his father. There had been a bust of Albert, Sr. at the University of Miami, but it had been stolen. Albert wrote Stanford that he wanted his (Stanford's) to be "a full bust on a marble pedestal." He added, "The one of my father need not be a full bust."

Ferrari made several trips to the University of Miami in connection with the busts and also for the sculpture which Albert saw he was commissioned to create for the building that was finally decided upon to bear the Pick name.

But earlier yet, on January 25, 1973, Albert was awarded an honorary Doctor of Laws by the University of Miami. The ceremony was meaningful to him for a number of reasons. One was the fact that he was participating in the same rite as his father, many years before. Another was the citation that mentioned not only his leadership in the business field (which already had taken a distinct secondary role in his thinking), his membership in the university's Society of University Founders, and his continued donations to the School of Music—in both cases following his father's lead—but also the two medals recently awarded him: the Eisenhower Medallion for his work with the People-to-People Program, and the U.S. Information Agency's Distinguished Service Award for outstanding services in advancing understanding and good will between peoples of the United States and other countries.

Since that concern with international relations had been the strongest motivation in his giving, aside from the theater he had built for Corinne, the emphasis on that part of his life pleased him enormously. The honorary doctorate was given "in recognition of his strong leadership in the fields of business, cultural and educational affairs of this nation, and of his contributions to international understanding." That put his activities in good perspective, he thought.

His feelings were reinforced on his role, as extensive as he could make it, in furthering the study of international relations, and his ties with the University of Miami. In April, 1974, he hosted a luncheon of corporate executives in Chicago as part of that university's fund drive; a gift to the university of $1,500 a few weeks later covered the luncheon costs. And on May 3, 1974, he pledged a gift of $200,000 to be used toward renovating an existing building on the campus of the University of Miami to be used as the Institute for Advanced International Studies. An original sculpture by Virginio Ferrari was to be placed in front of the building. Later, he pledged an additional $30,000, selling shares of stock to provide it, to pay for the Ferrari sculpture.

The project went smoothly, more smoothly than any he had yet initiated. Ralph Warburton, the University of Miami architect, kept Albert and Corinne informed of progress through his designs and renderings and letters; Stanford wrote regularly; the Development staff wrote frequently. A groundbreaking ceremony had been ruled out and the major event was the dedication, held on December 12, 1975.

But equally meaningful to Albert at that time were two letters he received. One was from Mose Harvey, the Director of the Center for Advanced International Studies, which referred specifically to the:

> help and especially the vision you and Corinne showed in conceiving the project as an integration of a building and a setting ... the architecture and the landscaped enclosed international garden create a happy blend of visual values set off most effectively by the truly outstanding sculpture by Virginio Ferrari that you so strongly encouraged us to commission.

Since Corinne had helped plan the landscaping, and Albert had hoped for an "integrated building in its own setting," he could not have been more satisfied.

The second letter was to "Dear mama and papa Pick" from Ferrari, written on December 19, 1974:

> Thank you for all that you have done for me and my family, for all that you have given me so generously. . . .
> I am very moved by the generous and spontaneous interest that you expressed for my family, my art. You have shown me in yourself more and more the beauty of being human.

The three universities bore buildings with the family name, and Albert had shown through it all his determination to contribute where and how he could, whatever the real and perceived obstacles. Ferrari's praise for his humanity was perhaps the perfect culmination: the physical structures he had helped build and the individuals he had touched in so doing had brought him to the highest peak of his active life.

The Highland Park, Illinois, home, bought in 1940.

Albert and Corinne on their yacht, Al-pho, 1968.

Corinne Frada Pick

Gladys Pick

Albert Pick III

Grandchildren of Albert and Corinne Pick: Paul
and Jenny Guggenheim (top), children of Gladys
Pick and Richard Guggenheim; Thomas and Janet
(center), children of Albert III and Faye Fitzgerald
Pick; Polly Ross (bottom), daughter of Gladys Pick
and William Ross.

Albert and Corinne at their fiftieth wedding anniversary, 1967.

13

A World to Discover

ALBERT and Corinne took their first trip to Europe in September, 1947. Early in their marriage, Albert, Sr., had given them a trip to Cuba; but they had not traveled since. Now, with the hotel chain prospering and the executive staff settled in to running an expanding, fast-paced company, they could look beyond winters in Florida and the rest of the year in their home in Highland Park.

They had moved to that northern suburb of Chicago in 1940, into a large, solid stone house of spacious rooms, high windows, carved moldings on the ceilings and gleaming oak trim on the stairway and walls in the double vestibule. Corinne had been scouting the North Shore of Chicago for some time, looking for the perfect house, since it was clear the little house on Cherry Street in Winnetka where they had lived since early in their marriage was too small for the kind of life they wanted to lead. Corinne had "jam sessions" of trios, quartets, and quintets in her living room with neighbors who played with the Chicago Symphony Orchestra; and she and Albert were beginning to make friends and entertain frequently. Also, there were the children.

Their daughter Gladys was born in 1927; and seven years

later a son, Albert III. They had waited a long time, and the children were greeted with excitement and a sense of satisfaction that there was another Pick family to continue the line. Albert had thought often of his brother and two sisters, long since dead, in the years when he was building a place for himself in the business and making a home with Corinne. He wanted a family of his own; he was the only one left to create one but, even more immediate, it had been a long time since he had been a part of a warm family unit. He would recall the nights when he and Laurence lay awake in their twin beds, whispering and laughing softly about the day's events; he would remember the sledding in the family's long sloping backyard on Prairie Avenue, the dancing classes attended by all his cousins, the Friday nights at Grandmother Dorshin's, the all-night parties with Laurence followed by six-A.M. golf games. He still smiled at memories of Pauline's indignance at being excluded from the code he and Laurence fabricated. With memories of his father's temper and the coolness between them mellowed by the passage of time, those years glowed in Albert's memory; and he knew that he wanted to recreate them to the extent that he could in his own home, his own family.

Certainly, his marriage was as good as he could ever have dreamed. He adored Corinne; he would to the day he died. He took enormous pleasure in her physical beauty and quick mind, the warmth of her personality that drew others to her as he had been drawn, and her considerable musical talents, which she used to liven their home and their evenings with friends as well as in recitals at the Georgian Hotel in Evanston and the Highland Park Music Club, the Chicago Music Club, and the Chicago Music Club of Women. Later, in their large home in Highland Park, they would host The Fine Arts String Quartet and the Chicago Symphony String Quartet at a "concerts in the home" series; and Corinne would record quintets with the group which consisted of players from the Chicago

Symphony Orchestra: Victor Aitay and Edgar Muenzer, violins, Milton Preeves, first viola, and Frank Miller, first cello of the Orchestra.

She gained in confidence through these friendships and recording sessions with established musicians. At first, new to marriage and the Pick family, she had been shy; there had been the years when Albert, Sr.'s dominance had threatened her marriage and she had fled, to be brought back by Albert. Those had been the years, too, when she was trying to understand the business that absorbed Albert's working hours: first the supply company, and then the Randolph Investment Company and the Pick Hotels.

She enrolled in courses at Northwestern University—to "catch up" with Albert, as she later said. At home she asked the meaning of words and phrases he used casually in conversation but was often made ashamed by his astonished, "Don't you know?" Finally, she girded herself; and the next time he put her down with his astonishment at her ignorance, she asked him what he would do if he went up to a policeman and asked directions to a street he had never seen. "What would you do," she asked, "if the policeman looked at you in amazement and asked, 'Don't you *know*?' "

Albert, caught in surprise at the picture she showed him of himself, apologized. For a moment, he had seen his father in himself, and he was upset. He would be more careful, he said, and he was, explaining to Corinne changes in the companies that changed his duties and responsibilities and the nation's economic climate that affected them as well.

Still, Corinne never became fully involved in the financial dealings of her husband's companies. When she became a member of the Board of Directors of the Pick Hotels, she concentrated on the decorating of new acquisitions and remodeling of hotels already held; she worked with decorators in this capacity, but she always saw her main function as being available to Albert as an ear and a commentator and support when he brought the world of business home at the end of the day.

Their marriage grew stronger with the years and with the birth of the children. Corinne would one day wonder if the extraordinary closeness between her and Albert, the passion that never flagged from the night they went to the theater and Albert proposed to her while parked beneath a street light in his mother's car, had not in a sense excluded the children, set them off center, shadowed beside the bright light of their parents' love. It may never have been so, but the fact that she conjectured about it many years after the children were grown, after Albert was dead, indicates the strength of that union that grew for nearly sixty years in joy and mutual pleasure.

The children did, of course, add to the joy. The house on Cherry Street was a happy place; and even business was made a part of the family, when Albert and Corinne took the children on automobile trips to inspect hotels in different states. In 1940, when the family moved to Highland Park in time for Gladys to begin high school, the new house became a center for school friends to gather; only a few blocks from the schools Gladys and Albert III attended, it was the first "stop-off" point when school let out for the day. In addition, and of no small note, the basement had a billiard room, a ping-pong room, and a refrigerator available to all who visited. Upstairs, listening to the laughter and lively conversation of high school boys and girls, first from Gladys's circle, and later from Albert III's, Corinne felt truly content amid beauty and comfort.

Both children were beautiful, Gladys with a dark striking beauty set off by porcelain skin, Albert III blond with a squared-off chin and strong face. He was a loved child and their home was warm and beautiful.

Corinne had hunted for a long time for the perfect house; the first requirement was that it have a living room large enough to hold two grand pianos at one end. (They had had to crawl under one piano to get to the dining room of the Cherry Street house.) She found the house in Highland Park, half a block from Lake Michigan on a large corner lot with huge old trees and wide expanses of velvety grass. Corinne and Albert had been guests in the one-hundred-year-old house, at parties given by the owners, Maurice and Maud Berkson. Albert was not sure he should spend the money for a new house in 1939, when the country was just struggling to pull itself out of the depression; but Berkson, sympathizing with Corinne's love of the house, urged them to take it and "pay when you can." They did, and they paid the full price within a few years. They stayed there the rest of their lives, in the elegance and comfort of its fifteen rooms and the ballroom on the third floor where Corinne sponsored art shows and which Gladys used as a studio when she was a student at the Art Institute.

As the children grew and Albert put the hotel chain on a firm foundation, he and Corinne began to think of travel. They had talked of it often; but, while the children were young, Corinne wanted to stay at home. When Albert visited hotels alone, or went to business meetings in New York and Miami, he would tuck something of Gladys' in his suitcase—a tiny bootie when she was a baby, or a picture she had drawn as she grew older—because he found it so difficult to be away. When Albert III was born, it became even harder; he had wanted, as Corinne later said, "a man child" for so long; the two of them had hoped for a boy through so many barren years that both were reluctant to be away for any long period of time.

But by 1947, Gladys was twenty and away at school; Albert III was at home with Walter Greenbolt and his wife who stayed in the Highland Park home, extending a business relationship into a personal one. That year, 1947, was the one in which Albert decided for the first time to attend the annual meeting of the International Hotel Association in London.

He had been a member of the American Hotel Association (later to become the American Hotel and Motel Association) since beginning his hotel chain, but his participation in the early years had been secondary to the work of building up his hotels and steering them through the chaos of the depression and the war years following. He began to hold offices in the AHA at the same time he turned his attention to the international association which, in spite of its name, had few American members and had never held an annual meeting in America.

Albert thought in terms of both a national and an international association; the hotels, he already saw, were a part of American "foreign policy" whether informal or not. European visitors to the United States after the war found hotels lacking in the basic services that their hotels on the continent provided —particularly translators (or, better still, bi-lingual and multi-lingual staff) and restaurants catering to a sophisticated and well-traveled clientele. It was clear to Albert that peace and prosperity, when it came to Europe through the Marshall Plan and new forms of industrialization which he could foresee, would increase the flow of Europeans to America; evidence of a flow in the other direction already was abundant. It would do no good, he told friends and business associates, to have a nation of hotels run by insular executives and untutored staffs. The time had come to think in terms of a worldwide network of hotels that would greet and smooth the way for visitors *from* all countries *to* all countries, and that also would act as an international "melting pot" for hotel executives to meet, to share ideas, and to become familiar with the customs of their fellow hotelmen in their various countries. These ideas naturally led to his participation in the People to People program; they also, more slowly and less directly, led to his philanthropic gifts in the field of international relations.

On that first trip to Europe, Albert plunged into his role, as he perceived it, as a representative of the United States and, simultaneously and nearly identically, as representative of an industry that dealt with "foreign relations" every day and would do so to a greater extent in the future. He and Corinne arrived in London during one of the first national strikes that paralyzed the country after the war. Wherever they went, from the time the *Mauritania* docked to the time they arrived for a luncheon with a number of Great Britain's business and hereditary elite, he saw signs of the strike covering, like a shadow, a land already shattered by war. That such a thing could happen to a people of bravery and courage infuriated him. He felt almost as if the strike were being visited upon him. He changed the theme of his luncheon speech before he rose to address the group.

It was an impressive occasion: the first formal banquet of many he and Corinne would attend in the next thirty years. The horseshoe table bore no signs of scarcity; it was elegantly set and lush with food. Each couple entering the room was announced with name and country of residence. The Prince of Wales and King Edward were toasted and Albert and Corinne each noted the fact to write in their reports for *Topicks*. When the meal was ended, they were told they could smoke. Then, before that quiet, well-bred, well-endowed group, many of whom would entertain Albert and Corinne at their estates in future years, Albert gave a speech that slashed at the strikers and what they were doing to "a great nation," saying:

> We share the responsibility for Europe's recovery and our shoulders are broad. But they are not broad enough to settle your strikes. This is something you have to settle for yourself—and it had better be soon.

He sat down to an ovation both he and Corinne would remember always. It did not matter that the audience was primed for such a speech, that another audience would have sat in stony silence or booed him; he had discovered his ability to move a group of people with his words, and he had done it in a foreign land as an American. It was a heady feeling. He looked at Corinne who smiled at him; she felt it too.

They spent the next six weeks in travel, discovering the old world which was new to them and which Albert had in effect made part of his province with his speech and with his determination to weld an international network of hotels. From Paris, they took train trips to Italy and Switzerland, hosted and guided by hotel committees in each country. There were banquets in their honor and tours to night clubs, restaurants, and local sights; in all, Albert and Corinne had seven weeks to discover Europe. They returned on the *Queen Elizabeth,* thoroughly dedicated travelers, committed to a return visit. In fact, they would make over thirty more trips.

Most of the trips were made in conjunction with annual meetings of the International Hotel Association. Some were vacations, as the Hawaii trip of 1949, which Albert described in *Topicks*; and one to South America was planned around a meeting of the National Board of Trustees of the People-to-People organization in Guadalajara and Mexico City, Mexico. (Through an introduction, they were invited to visit Queen Fredericka of Greece in her summer palace; they went to Buckingham Palace for the photograph promised by Prince Philip on his visit to La Rabida.)

As Albert and Corinne became experienced travelers, both wrote long descriptions of their experiences and thoughts for publication in *Topicks,* and Corinne became a skilled photographer, carrying one or two cameras into caves, to the peaks of mountains, on bumpy airplane trips in small chartered planes swooping over otherwise inaccessible valleys and mountain ranges. The two of them were indefatigable, endlessly curious, unashamed of being tourists in strange lands. They had a wonderful time.

A break came in the travel-and-association schedule when their daughter Gladys was married to William Ross on September 29, 1950. The wedding was lavish; and Albert beamed at the two beautiful women he loved, his wife and daughter, and the four hundred guests who crowded the Pick-Congress Gold Room.

That marriage would founder; but the occasion, like the celebration of "100 Years of Service to Hoteldom" in the same room three years earlier, was witness to Albert's position in Chicago's business and social circles. If he was not a prime mover, he was in the circle that wielded economic influence. Later, he would be lauded for philanthropic activities at La Rabida Sanitorium, and the Universities of Chicago and Miami and Northwestern University; but in 1950, at the beginning of the long curve of his most successful years, he already was being watched as one who bore a well-known name and, on his own, was giving it added importance in the business world.

His parents were not with him to witness either of the events that symbolized his solidified position in these different worlds. Gertrude had died in 1945. Besides the grief of loss, Albert had felt the last warm, living tie between him and his father break. Gertrude's sweetness and lively imagination had bridged, over and over again, the angry gulfs of silence between the two men; when she had failed to do so, she had still remained a loving and loved touchstone. In a sense, in many of the aspects of their relationship over the years, Albert and his father had circled each other around the pivot that was Gertrude. After her death, Albert, Sr., barely spoke to or communicated with his son for five years, though he kept in touch with Corinne.

Albert, Sr., married again in five years; and it was his new wife, Florence Torrico Pick, who attended Gladys's wedding. He was not feeling well, he told Corinne; it was the beginning of the period when he would withdraw more and more, in part from physical ills, in part from depression over Gertrude's death, over the letting-go of his beloved real estate dealings, over his anger at his son that he did not know how to handle now that it was diminishing in the face of his other problems.

He brooded for five years, isolated by age and weariness from much of the life of Miami Beach, his new wife becoming entrenched in the city's social life as he withdrew. He was alone a great deal. Finally, on Albert's sixtieth birthday in 1955, Albert, Sr., picked up the telephone to call his son and give him good wishes to repair the damage of many of those sixty years.

Corinne had written him about the lavish weekend party she had planned in which 300 guests would be put up at the Pick-Congress for dinner, entertainment, and socializing; he called the hotel, had Albert paged and talked for a long time while Albert listened.

"I'm recasting my life," he said, meaning, Albert understood, that everything was under review. "I admire you for what you've done; I want you to know that. I admire you for what you've done with your life in spite of my obstacles. I congratulate you. I congratulate you on your birthday and on your life. And I send you my love."

The noises of the party crowded in on Albert; he closed the door. "I'm a very lonely man," his father said. "Florence is out a great deal of the time; she has a heavy social life. I'm alone so much. I see almost no one."

Albert mentioned a few names of old friends; where were they? His father responded shortly: some were dead; others had faded from his life. "You've been gracious to me," he went on, as if the interruption had not occurred. "You could have told me to go to hell a dozen or more times, but you never did. I wouldn't have been surprised if you had, but you never did. That makes me very happy. You make me proud and happy. Will you come to see me? I've lost a son and two daughters, and then I threw you out of my life; it was a terrible mistake. I need you. Please come to see me."

Albert hesitated. There were so many emotions to be sorted out. Finally, he suggested his father come to Chicago. "Spend the summer with us," he said. "Miami in July is so hot; we'll give you your own suite in the house and a car and chauffeur. Come any time you want."

His father argued. "I can't. I don't have the strength. The house here is air conditioned. Please come."

Albert temporized. "We could come in September."

His father sighed. "And we can talk on the telephone until then?"

"Whenever you want," Albert said. "You've made this a very special day for me."

A week later, on July 9, 1955, Albert, Sr., age 86 years, died in his home in Miami Beach.

When Albert, Jr., was nearly the age at which his father had died, he would recall their last conversation as his "most treasured memory" of his father. He could describe a father he had known as a youth and a businessman: Albert, Sr., was, he said, imaginative, strong-willed, an excellent merchant, and a man of good taste; but also a difficult man: a martinet. The tensions had faded over the years, but they never disappeared until his father was dead; then he could deliver an obituary that was as objective as a man could make it of another whose life had entwined his own in stress for so long. And that he could balance his feelings about his father was shown most clearly in the fact that he retained the "Jr." after his name until the end of his life; he saw no reason to drop it simply because his father was dead.

Besides, his name, his full name, was known and respected. Two events were signs of the level he had reached in that regard. The first was the role he played in the presidential nomination of 1952 which led, indirectly, to the position he came to hold in the People-to-People movement. He had been an observer and host for the presidential nominating convention, held in Chicago that year, and his friend Robert Taft, senator from Ohio, was a guest in the Pick-Congress. Taft had been the attorney for the Ohio hotels owned by the Pick chain; he and Albert became friends and, with their wives, they celebrated occasions together when Albert and Corinne were in Ohio. One, recalled by Albert as one of his most pleasant birthdays, was his fifty-seventh, celebrated at dinner in the Pick-Congress with the Tafts as his and Corinne's guests.

The campaign between Dwight Eisenhower and Robert Taft for the Republican nomination seemed to Albert to be a particularly vicious one, with what he called later "some of the worst mud-slinging" he had ever seen. He thought it shameful that that would go on between Republicans. Albert, through friendship and a close sympathy with his conservative politics, supported Taft; he had contributed to his campaign and offered him a suite in the Pick-Congress for the convention. He had little close knowledge of Eisenhower beyond his disgust with what he called the "antics" of Eisenhower's publicists; his support of Taft was a positive, rather than an anti-Eisenhower, position.

So it was that, when the tenor of the convention became clear—that the nomination would go to Eisenhower—Albert saw himself as a peacemaker. He was close to Taft and had a number of good friends in the Republican party; for many years, he had contributed to Republican causes, and through them he had met Herbert Brownell, Eisenhower's campaign manager and the man whom Eisenhower would designate Attorney General upon his election.

Eisenhower was staying in a suite at the Conrad Hilton Hotel, a few blocks from the Pick-Congress. Albert went to see Brownell there and offered his congratulations on what seemed to be certain victory when the balloting resumed that evening. "It looks like you'll win," he said, "and we'll all stand behind the General." Then he offered to "come over to the other camp." Senator Taft, he suggested, would come to Eisenhower and offer his congratulations and support in person. Brownell was enthusiastic about the idea. Later, Albert suggested a change: that "Ike would walk over to the Pick-

Congress and ask for Senator Taft's support." Brownell supported the change.

Albert walked back to the Pick-Congress to give Taft the schedule for that night, after the balloting but before Eisenhower's appearance in the Amphitheater. He called Chicago's television stations, giving each "advance notice" of the meeting. Then, he joined Corinne in the room they had taken for the duration of the convention. Together, they watched the balloting that led to Eisenhower's nomination; together they watched the dramatic moment when Eisenhower walked into Senator Taft's hotel suite and clasped his hand, asking for his support in the campaign to come. Others in the room with Albert and Corinne commented on the magnanimity, even the grandeur, of the gesture. Albert watched in silence and was silent in the days that followed, when Herbert Brownell received congratulations for conceiving the idea and carrying it out. He held the truth inside him, not bitterly but proudly; he and Corinne carried it with them to Washington for the inauguration where they were guests of the Brownells, sitting in their box at the Inaugural Ball and going to a round of parties with them.

Eisenhower met Albert and Corinne in his box at the Inaugural Ball. He knew of Albert as a staunch supporter of the Republican Party; the two men talked briefly about some of the issues on which Eisenhower had been elected. Eisenhower, Corinne recalled years later, "looked me up and down" boldly; he admired good-looking women and made no secret of it. Later, when Eisenhower came to Chicago, he invited Albert to one of the early planning sessions at Gettysburg in 1956 when People-to-People was being organized. The friendship with Eisenhower was one of Albert's most satisfying in a long list of good friendships; and when Eisenhower died in 1969, he wrote a tribute in his regular editorial space in *Topicks* that said in part:

Mr. Eisenhower lived life to its fullest and left behind him an enviable record of greatness. He was a man of courage, a man of the highest integrity, a religious man, and a man of peace—truly a man of *all* seasons.

Another event took place about the time of the Eisenhower inauguration which marked Albert's business life: in 1953, having worked on committees and a number of hotel projects for several years, Albert was elected president of the American Hotel Association at its forty-second annual convention in Montreal. He had taken a contingent with him from Chicago—almost one hundred hotel managers and home office executives with their wives went as his guests for the four-day convention, traveling on six special cars of the Grand Trunk and Western railroad line.

Albert spoke at the installation luncheon—his first speech as president of the association—surveying the industry and its future and outlining, as well, changes he thought were due in the association itself. He had long wanted to encourage more participation among the members, to broaden the scope of activities initiated and conducted by the membership. Just as he preferred working with individuals to dealing with committees and institutionalized procedures, so he wanted to work in an organization made up of working members rather than of a few strong committee chairman who, by default, *became* the organization. He expected some resistance to his platform of change, and he got it; but there was support from a number of committee chairmen and members who had been chafing at the difficulty of making themselves heard. It was not a fight—more a struggle of ideas—but he was pleased when, over a period of months, there were visible changes in the numbers of members involved in decision-making and the quality of activities undertaken in such fields as personnel hiring and training, financial management, food service, and insurance, among a long list he studied and enlarged.

At the same time, he created and headed a committee that

formulated scholarship plans for students in hotel schools and other ways in which the association could work to help young people move through the educational process into hotel management. The same committee created a credit card system for the American Hotel Association (later purchased by American Express). It was, he felt, one of the most productive of the association's working groups.

He headed the association with the kind of gentle humor punctuated by flashing wit for which he was becoming known. It was exemplified one night in an incident retold at dozens of meetings in years following. The featured speaker at a regional dinner meeting of hotel managers, Albert sat at the head table through hours of droning reports and self-aggrandizing monologues; he was restless on the hard seat and, looking at Corinne at the table just below his, he saw that she was not only restless but tired and becoming angry. He was introduced at a little before midnight, in another overlong speech, and finally stood to face the impatient audience.

"Ladies and gentlemen," he said mildly, with barely a twinkle in his eye. "I was scheduled to speak to you on Saturday night. It is now Sunday morning. Therefore, let me announce the date of our next meeting to you and conclude." He did so and sat down to thunderous applause.

Yet he took the association very seriously, as he took the more ceremonial, less directly influential, International Hotel Association. The work he did and the people he met, both as officer, president, and past president, all contributed, he felt, to the strength of the hotel industry. And for many years that was his major concern.

The next year, in the November following his sixtieth birthday and his father's death, he began to work for changes in the American hoteliers' attitude toward European hotels. Until then, it could best be characterized as complete disinterest. He proposed to the AHA Board of Directors that they interest American hotel people in joining him at the IHA biennial congress in Rome. He had thought about this for some time, he said; it was important that Americans become "peace ambassadors" who would participate in international conventions, thus showing that they were interested in "devoting their own time, and spending their own money, not only for their own business purposes, but also in the interests of international good will and understanding."

With the support of the AHA board, he went to Washington, making appointments with officials of the Foreign Operations Administration and the Departments of State and Commerce. He described his program, gave officials copies of the objectives as he had written them, and left with enthusiastic praise ringing in his ears for his unofficial "ambassadorship." Later, Secretary of State John Foster Dulles, Governor Harold Stassen, then director of the Foreign Operations Administration, Secretary of Commerce Sinclair Weeks, and President Dwight D. Eisenhower all sent letters of commendation and encouragement.

It was a time of great excitement for Albert and for Corinne, who saw him stepping into new arenas with the same commitment he gave to all his activities—and the same enthusiasm. He recruited nearly one hundred hotelmen and their wives as delegates and members of the AHA to go with him to Rome and from there to other cities of Europe, acting as goodwill ambassadors wherever they went.

Albert wrote a description for *Topicks* of the cocktail party at the Waldorf-Astoria in New York City, where he:

> passed out red-white-and-blue identification badges to our delegates, and made a talk to them, advising that . . . I hoped each and every one of them would take unto himself the personal duty and responsibility of meeting as many Europeans, both hotelmen and others, as they could—learning about their country, their interests and problems, and telling them about the United States. I stressed the urgency of reiterating our objectives of world peace, international good will

and understanding, and inviting them to come and see our country—to visit us in our hotels, see our big cities and small towns, view our national capital, national parks, and other places of historic interest.

About fifteen hundred delegates from forty-three countries attended the Congress; speeches were translated simultaneously into French, Italian, English, and Spanish. When he spoke, Albert read excerpts from the letters he had received from Eisenhower, Dulles, Stassen, and Weeks; he emphasized his concerns with international travel as "a proper approach to understanding the peace." Later, he participated in a number of small sessions that worked on reducing red tape at national borders, smoothing customs inspections, clarifying details of currency exchange and other facets of international travel that could make or mar trips for travelers. Albert found it all absorbing and stimulating, because he could relate it to the theme of his trip: everything was made a part of the movement for world peace through understanding, all of which could be helped by increasing the flow of international travel. The three poles of his speech and of his work in both the American and the International Hotel Associations—travel, understanding, peace— would become his hallmarks, and would play a large role in the buildings he built on university campuses for the study of international relations.

He and Corinne stayed on in Rome for a few days, glorying in the vastness of scenes they had known until then only in books. Geneva and Paris followed; hosted by hotelmen, they saw the best of Europe, through soccer games, night clubs, superb restaurants, the finest hotels, and visits in private homes. The trip set the pattern for all those that would follow, with the exception of two that broke new ground for them. One was to the Soviet Union and Eastern Europe in 1954, arranged by Carter Davidson, president of the Chicago Council on Foreign Relations. On that trip, in Brussels, Albert complained to the hotel clerk about the dismal room they had been given;

and the manager, on reading the Pick Hotels card Albert handed him, transferred them to a suite with the beds on a platform for a superb view through the window. The rest of the trip, on which they were joined by their son Albert III and a friend, was handled by Intourist, through Poland, the Soviet Union, and Czechoslovakia. As with all their trips, they crammed the hours and the days, often going twenty hours at a stretch to meet as many people as they could while, with her camera, Corinne recorded hundreds upon hundreds of buildings, faces, and scenes.

The other trip to break the pattern of yearly tours of Europe was in connection with the annual meeting of the International Hotel Association Executive Council in 1961 in Tel Aviv, Israel. The business meeting came at the end of a tour of the Far East that led from Japan to Hong Kong, Thailand, India, Greece, and thence to Israel. Corinne kept notes and a diary, describing everything they saw, ate, and heard, and the people they met.

In every city, they examined the hotels, particularly with regard to possible leasing or management arrangements for Pick Hotels, but also to keep a record of places they could suggest to others as a part of the People to People program. Albert, in fact, saw himself as much a representative of that cause—of world peace and understanding—as he was of his hotels; and in business meetings, he distributed copies of the booklet, "A Guide for Guests from Abroad in American Hotels," which he had sponsored through the American Hotel and Motel Association. Printed in five languages (and, after the Far East tour, in Japanese), the booklets were part of the Travel U.S.A. program that in turn was one aspect of "Travel to the U.S.A. Year" designated by Dwight Eisenhower for 1960.

It had been Eisenhower who conceived the People to People movement in 1956. In a People-to-People meeting at his Gettysburg farm, he had said:

Almost anybody can be a good general; it's not that that gives me satisfaction today. What pleases me most is that I began the People-to-People movement; that is something that gives hope for the future.

Eisenhower had articulated the goals of People-to-People as a program that:

... should be, on our side, an effort to learn more about and understand our fellows, accompanied by an expanding crusade to portray the American way, the American system, the American people ... in all areas of our national being, cultural and intellectual, recreational and social, professional and economic.
So doing, we shall help the world's people to achieve mutual understanding based on truth proudly and fully exposed.

With the financial backing of Joyce Hall of Hallmark Greeting Cards, the movement gathered momentum, as representatives of business, industry, entertainment, and social organizations gathered for a White House organizing conference and set up committees to conduct the business of the movement through the months between annual general meetings. In 1961, the movement became a corporation, non-profit, non-governmental, non-political, with then President John F. Kennedy as honorary chairman and General Eisenhower as Chairman of the Board of Trustees. It sponsored foreign tours by American scientists, educators, and farmers, instituted letter exchanges between Americans and "pen pals" in Europe, organized foreign tours for American sports teams and the reverse as well, arranged for housing for foreign students on American campuses, and was involved in a number of other such projects. At various times, the organization claimed world-wide membership ranging from the hundreds of thousands to the millions; whatever its true membership, it generated a great deal of attention on the goals it had set itself.

Albert subscribed fervently to those goals: America, he

believed, held up to the world as model and example not only would create good will, but also would increase understanding of its motives and way of life. And that way led the path to peace and harmony in the world. He believed that in the 1950s, when his involvement with People-to-People was just beginning; he believed it far more strongly in the 1960s, when his world trips had given him a chance to discover the many facets of cultures and countries that, he knew, had to be understood and accommodated if peace were to be a reality.

He had first been asked to serve on the hotel committee of People-to-People; in 1958, he was on the Board of Trustees and co-chairman with Herbert Blunck, of Washington, D.C., of the People to People Committee of the American Hotel and Motel Association. His major role, as he saw it, was to promote international travel: to convince Europeans and Asians that America would welcome them with comfort, convenience, hospitality and an array of attractions. To this end, he supported the use of multi-language printed materials on hotels and features of American life; he led the effort that resulted in international-symbol directional signs in hotels; he saw to it, when he could, that the AH&MA made a yearly contribution to People to People as its part in promotion within the larger organization; and he "pushed" People-to-People at hotel meetings around the world, making it known to hotel men and women and encouraging them to join.

He was able to enlist large groups to accompany him and Corinne to international meetings; and, in December, 1956, after months of pressure, he managed to bring the International Hotel Association to America for its first Congress ever outside Europe. The Congress was held in Washington, D.C., with Albert the chairman; amid a dozen events, including a concert by the National Symphony at the Mayflower Hotel, the organizers hosted a traditional American Thanksgiving dinner for the six hundred hotelmen. Albert's message as chairman closed with "the hope that, from your meetings and contacts with us, many lasting friendships will result, and that warmer relationships and still greater mutual understanding will accrue to the peoples and governments of the free world."

He carried the same message to other meetings in South America and Mexico, where he also made clear that he, and the American Hotel and Motel Association through him, would make trips to the United States smooth and memorable for visitors.

He was, himself, as good a visitor as a host. He and Corinne knew how to discover a country by air, land, and sea—by donkey and by rail car, if need be. From a ship passing through the Panama Canal to explorations of caves to a small, chartered plane swooping low over the live Chilean volcano Vilarica, Corinne snapped photographs and Albert kept notes. The trip was a brilliant one in large part because of their unsleeping curiosity and intrepidity.

In 1969, as he was becoming deeply involved in his philanthropic activities at the University of Chicago, Northwestern University, and the University of Miami, he had less time for People-to-People. Much of his participation then was by mail; he followed the meetings by reading the minutes which were sent to him and commenting upon them to appropriate people who, he thought, could strengthen various aspects of the organization and its work.

In a letter of October 31, 1969, to William Popham of San Francisco, Albert outlined much of his philosophy on People-to-People and the role the hotel industry could play, not only in the People-to-People organization, but in the world at large. By that date, the committee within the hotel association had been renamed the International Travel Committee to tie it more closely to the industry; but Albert never wavered in his belief that People-to-People should be an integral part of all the Travel Committee's activities. He wrote to Popham:

> I feel we should keep our identity with the People-to-People movement. Certain of the original committees are

still very active—such as the People-to-People Health Foundation with its Project Hope which as you probably know involves a large ship manned with doctors and nurses sailing around the world performing surgery, teaching local doctors and nurses, dispensing medicine, literature, etc., the national music committee; sports; pen-pal committee where many thousands from the United States form "writing" friendships with people of foreign lands; sister city programs where certain cities in our country are teamed with cities of similar importance abroad; etc.

The objectives of the International Travel People-to-People Committees are well known to all, and have been very well discussed in previous meetings, so I feel the most important thing is really to implement our established policy of being as helpful as possible in promoting travel to our country, cooperating with the government and any other proper agency, and then, when and if the international traveler visits us, that we do everything possible to make their [sic] stay with us interesting and enjoyable, and do what we can to promote international friendship and understanding. Never in my lifetime was this more important than now.

It is my opinion that the International Travel People-to-People Committee is of greater and greater importance in the hotel industry as international travel grows and world tensions and conflicts seem to proliferate. Therefore I feel the committee should have its own identity and its own meeting.

As a result of his letters and conversations with members of the International Travel Committee and the larger membership, the American Hotel and Motel Association, through its American Hotel Foundation, continued yearly donations to People to People long after Albert had ended his active participation. He considered its financial support one of his most enduring contributions. But there was one other: Corinne, too, had been elected a Trustee of People-to-People; and, after his death, she continued to play a role in its meetings and activities.

Two awards came to Albert through his involvement with

People-to-People and his efforts to bring foreign visitors to the United States. In 1962, the Pick Hotels Corporation was awarded the Presidential "E" Award with a citation that read:

The Pick Hotels Corporation has done outstanding work with overseas societies and airlines to attract group tours of European business and professional organizations in the United States. An imaginative advertising campaign and an energetic sales program, promoting fixed-cost rates and multi-lingual hotel services, brought 199 groups from 29 countries to the U.S. in nine months, a total of more than 33,000 overseas visitors. This achievement has led to a better understanding of the United States and our private enterprise system abroad and represents a significant contribution to the export expansion program.

Albert could point with pride to the figures that lay behind the citation: when he began his efforts to bring foreign visitors to the United States in 1960, the Pick Hotels greeted 2,500 guests from overseas. Two years later, the figure was 33,000; and by 1965, it approached 100,000, mainly through trade delegations from Europe. The "E" (standing for Excellence in developing export sales and interesting tourists in coming to the United States) was one recognition of a program in all the Pick hotels that included foreign language guides for guests and tour conductors, multi-lingual employees, foreign language menus, special foods and wines, reduced guaranteed rates for rooms and meals to be economically compatible with overseas prices, advertising in foreign publications, and lobby signs in international symbols or foreign languages.

Of even greater note to Albert, because of his strong feeling of loyalty and affection for Dwight Eisenhower, was the award of an Eisenhower Medallion on December 1, 1972. The award was made by Mrs. Mamie Eisenhower at a ceremony in the International Club, Washington, D.C., during the annual meeting of People-to-People International. In his acceptance speech, Albert reiterated his dedication to international communication and cooperation:

Some day let us hope and pray that all wars will end and that people the world over will live in peace and security. We look to the day when small countries may exist in peace, free from any threats from their larger and more powerful neighbors. I personally deem it a privilege to have been able to serve in this most worthwhile endeavor. . . . I hope to be of more help, and for the entire People-to-People movement I ask your continuing interest and efforts so that it can be even more effective.

The years of Albert's participation in People-to-People were the years in which he was most active, often simultaneously and in overlapping trips, in the American Hotel and Motel Association and the International Hotel Association. They were good years, crowded with friends in America and in countries throughout Europe and with the satisfying knowledge that the hotel chain was prospering.

His work in the hotel field had been recognized as had his work with People-to-People: in April of 1955, he had been named "Hotel Man of the Year" for 1954, and his name was enrolled in the Hall of Distinction at Michigan State College in East Lansing, Michigan. The award, given annually, was made by Michigan State and the Founders Fund in acknowledgement of "distinguished and unusual service to the hotel industry."

That hotel award, coupled with an award eight years later, in 1963, for his work with La Rabida Hospital, represented for him the poles of his life: success in the business world and dedication to the humanitarian one. The La Rabida award was the presentation to Albert of a bound volume of published research on rheumatic disease. The scientific staff of the hospital dedicated it to Albert; and it was presented to him by Albert Dorfman, Director of Research. Though it did not need reiterating, many said that night that such research would not have been possible without the support of Albert and the others whom he brought into the "fold" of La Rabida.

The awards and the many forms of personal recognition that

came to Albert in these years were of great significance to him, but they were only elements in a lifetime that was founded on his marriage to Corinne—harmonious, deeply loving, filled with mutual pleasure in each other.

There were many visible signs of the strength of their marriage, but the most festive was their fiftieth wedding celebration in the Gold Room of the Pick Congress on December 27, 1967, with four hundred guests, a string orchestra, and dinner on gold-bedecked tables. There had been a previous special anniversary, a double celebration of Albert and Corinne's twenty-fifth and Albert, Sr., and Gertrude's 50th wedding anniversaries, both on December 27, 1942. The party was at Albert and Gertrude's home in Miami Beach; it was, for the Picks, a small affair with only fifty people, in part because the war made travel difficult and time off impossible for many. But it was cause for joy and special acknowledgement, not only of a milestone but also of relationships that, through pain, sorrow, and difficult times, had survived. To mark the specialness of the day, Corinne designed and sewed by hand two full-length dresses, a gold one for Gertrude and a silver one for herself. The dresses symbolized the relationship of the two women as much as the numerical anniversaries. Gertrude was not well in these last years of her life (she died in 1945) and Corinne was more a daughter to her now than at times in the past when Dorothy and Pauline were alive and Corinne absorbed in building a good foundation for her own marriage. She and Gertrude had become friends as well as "mother-daughter" and when the gold and silver dresses were folded away after the celebration it was in acknowledgement that the relationship would live, though the dresses would only be treasured as a focus for memory, not to be worn again. They never were.

Gertrude and Albert, Sr., were gone by the time Albert and Corinne marked their 50th anniversary; Corinne's dress this time was white worked with beads and sequins; and Albert, as all the men, including his seven year-old-grandson, was in tuxedo. Albert and Corinne recalled that other anniversary, but the events of this one swept them up. It was a time of articulating what their friends had felt; it was a time when the full measure of the couple could be taken in one place in one evening, for it was a time when all their many worlds came together: family, business, artistic, and, though the major gifts were still to be made, philanthropic—through the presence of Edward Levi, president-elect of the University of Chicago, Fairfax Cone, Chairman of that university's Board of Trustees, and Lawrence Kimpton, former chancellor of the university.

The measure of Albert and Corinne was seen in the speeches made to them. The first was given by Dr. Preston Bradley, pastor of the People's Church of Chicago, a longtime close friend:

> Albert and Corinne. . . . We love you. We are grateful that, in a world bewitched by racial hatred and religious bigotries, there are those who live among us who rise out of the depths to the high plateaus of love, brotherhood, and understanding. . . .

Lawrence Kimpton, who had known Albert through the University of Chicago Board of Trustees and then had become friend and nearly a family member over the years, spoke to the guests about the shared characteristics of Albert and Corinne. One was their sense of humor he said, and then:

> The second shared characteristic is what brings all of us here this evening. They have dedicated their lives to each other, to their friends, and to humanity. There is no one here this evening who has not been touched by their kindness, thoughtfulness, and generosity.
>
> And we have also been touched and benefited by their goodness. It is peculiarly fitting, at this season of the year, when we think most of children and our friends and of our yearning for world understanding and peace, that we should celebrate the fiftieth anniversary of the marriage of Albert and Corinne.

Kimpton also had described Albert and Corinne's *non*-sharing as a contribution to their marriage:

> Corinne is an artist. She would have been a great concert pianist if she had devoted herself to music instead of to Albert.
>
> And Albert, dear Albert, I don't think he could carry a tune in a tub, if I may say so respectfully. He's a businessman and a good one.
>
> I remember his telling me once as a surprise that he had given Corinne some stock and she had not even looked at the day's quotation to determine its value. How could anyone behave like that? Marvelously, these two diverse temperaments have learned to supplement each other over fifty years in what I can only call a divine marital orchestration. Playing different instruments, they make sweet music in their respect and tenderness for each other.

Sharing and non-sharing, Albert and Corinne smiled at each other. And at the end of the speeches, they turned to each other, Albert saying to Corinne that it had "taken me almost this long to swallow the lump in my throat. . . . I have never seen you look lovelier nor more radiant than tonight. . . ."

And Corinne clasped her hands and said, "To my darling, . . . with his generous heart and wise understanding, go my love and gratitude for making life for me such a glorious adventure. Thank you."

In a lifetime of love and companionship, it was a rare moment of public intimacy shared with a large crowd of affectionate family and friends. It typified all the best of their good years together.

14

Milestones and Memories

O N JULY 2, 1970, Albert stepped off the Highland Park commuter train when it pulled into the Chicago and North Western station and was greeted by his three top corporation officers, who escorted him on the ten-minute walk to his office. A red carpet extended from the curbing through the lobby to a sign beside the elevators. The sign congratulated "Albert Pick, Jr., on [his] diamond birthday anniversary."

Seventy-five years. He was robust, handsome, his hair and mustache white, his eyes clear and piercing as ever. He looked back on those seventy-five years as prologue to what still lay ahead: the gifts, then in the planning stage, to three universities, more travels, the work he did as member of several boards of trustees, a full social life with friends in all parts of the world, more time with Corinne.

On this day, a number of tributes made him aware of his place in the city. Radio stations WGN (owned and operated by the *Chicago Tribune*, and WNUS, a suburban station whose listening area included Highland Park, both paid him on-the-air tributes; the columnists of the four Chicago newspapers (the *Tribune*, the *Chicago Sun-Times*, *Chicago Today*, and the *Chicago Daily News;* the latter two would be shut down in later years) printed birthday greetings, and *Chicago Tribune* financial editor Nick Poulos wrote a feature interview for the business section.

Albert discussed the hotels and his intention to remain active in the corporation in the Poulos interview. Asked whether he planned to expand the chain overseas, he shook his head. "We're comforted by the fact that we operate solely in the United States," he said. "We don't want any part of the problems abroad. We're just as happy catering to people from abroad visiting the United States." Nor was he interested in having the chain become the largest in the country. "Bigness as such is not desirable. Our organization is not so big that we lose sight of the individual employee or customer."

More important, he was concerned about the quality of management: that which makes or breaks a company. He would not expand his chain beyond the corporation's ability to finance expansion, because "Lenders want an equity interest—a piece of the action—in return for financing. Well, they won't get it from me. Lenders belong in the lending business, not the hotel business. I think it's economically hazardous to do business that way. It's not a healthy situation." He was sole stockholder in the Pick Hotels Corporation; he had held out against the importuning of others and his own cautionary thoughts, and he would not change now.

He had articulated these ideas in previous years in different forums. He had been interviewed by the major Chicago newspapers since the 1950s, when the hotel chain was reaching for its position as the third largest privately owned chain in the country. In 1963, he was named "Businessman of the Day" by Mid-America Federal Savings and Loan Association in its regular feature of that name on radio station WAIT. And in May of 1964, he participated in "The Albert Pick Story" on the *Executive '64* series on radio station WMAQ (NBC), a program that dramatized the family's early years in

Chicago and concluded with a panel discussion with Albert, his long-time attorney and friend Alan Altheimer, and Albert Dorfman. Besides the regular Sunday night airing, the tape was broadcast to schools throughout the area, which gave Albert special pleasure. He already was thinking of ways he could support and strengthen education; this was one of his first experiences "in school."

He was an established, settled figure in the many worlds in which he moved, as the dramatization of his family's involvement with Chicago, from Civil War days on, showed. And he was five times a grandfather, which gave him special pleasure, as he had forged strong bonds with the children of his children and his sense of continuity was more sure than ever.

Gladys had remarried in 1955; her husband, Richard Guggenheim, became another "son" to Corinne and Albert, who grew very close to him over the years. (The wedding was held in Albert and Corinne's living room, one of three such family weddings that led to the dubbing of the room as "the Pick Marriage Chapel." One wedding linked Gertrude Pick—Pauline's daughter who had been raised by Albert, Sr., and Gertrude after Pauline's death—and Robert Lesman. Gertrude Lesman became "daughter" and friend to Albert and Corinne, especially in Albert's last illness.) Pauline, Gladys' first child, named for Albert's sister, was at the Highland Park house frequently; and when Gladys and Guggenheim had two more children, Paul and Jeanette (the latter named for Albert's grandmother), the threesome attached themselves to Corinne and Albert, as the young often do with older generations, in a close and loving friendship that Albert treasured, especially as he became ill.

The children were like their mother in vivacity and beauty, and in grace as well. Gladys had directed aqua shows and choral groups in high school and later studied art for two years at the Chicago Art Institute; these she passed on to her children, who would bring news of college, ski trips, boating, and all their passions to the grandparents who, they knew, would welcome their tales.

Albert III had been graduated from college in 1956, having been both president of his fraternity and the same restless, eager student as the boy who had said, years before, when told he was too young to have a drivers license, "Mother, why didn't you have me sooner?" He had worked in the hotel corporation for seven years before leaving to work with a brokerage firm; like his father, he was happiest when dealing with finances. His two children by his first wife, Thomas and Janet, joined the group in Albert and Corinne's house to form what Albert called the "great invention" of grandchildren. The young voices and the clear eyes of these children, running in and out as if the house were theirs, made him feel a complete family man; and he understood a long-ago letter of his father's from Miami, singing the praises of Gladys as a baby when they cared for her for a month.

In business, as in family matters, he felt in control. He had been interviewed on the occasion of his seventieth birthday, in addition to the others, by then financial editor of the *Chicago Tribune* William Clark. At that time, asked how many stockholders were in the Pick Hotels Corporation, he had "raised a single, eloquent finger," Clark wrote. At the same time, to Clark's questions about his activities within and outside the corporation, Albert had said, "I want gradually to move into a still-interested-but-not-so-completely-involved relationship with some of these. I want to be a little more footloose, though I have no notion of retiring."

To a large extent, he had done that. The 1970s were the years of building on campuses (handled mostly through correspondence) and extended travel to new and familiar countries. He was indeed more "footloose" than before. Yet he maintained contact with the organizations he had served as trustee, and his checkbook was always ready when they needed help or told him of others in need.

He found it difficult to refuse requests for help, especially when he could see the individuals who would benefit. As trustee of Highland Park Hospital during the years when it was planning major expansions, he toured the corridors and patients' rooms so that he could translate board discussions into human terms, and dollars into human needs.

He had done so with other hospitals as well. His most significant and long-term contributions—in time and energy, as well as money—were to La Rabida, which had tugged at his heart since he first visited it. The sick children there may well have reminded him of his brother Laurence, but he was concerned for children in general and especially the poor who had nowhere to go but such hospitals as this which set aside funds for patients who could pay nothing. In addition, he admired the doctors and nurses on the staff who gave so much of themselves to keep the hospital functioning through difficult times when funds were low and public interest negligible. Albert's efforts, called "determining" by those involved, to bring about an affiliation between La Rabida and the University of Chicago were one of his most important and enduring legacies, ensuring stability to the hospital and a strong foundation for future research in rheumatic fever and other diseases of children.

But he did not confine his attention to La Rabida. The concerns that had led there underlay other gifts. In this, he followed his father. Albert, Sr., toward the end of his life, had endowed a Negro hospital in Miami with funds set aside for those who, in those years before the federal government had begun its medicaid and medicare programs, could not otherwise afford hospital care. Albert's concerns were broader: he wanted the poor to have access to health and education that would help lift them from their poverty. Scholarships to over fifteen different colleges and universities were one expression of that concern: from the music school of Northwestern University, where the annual Corinne Frada Pick Scholarship was awarded to a promising musician, to general funds such as the United Negro College Fund and the Ohio Foundation of Independent Colleges, to specially targeted gifts such as those to the Culinary Institute of America for restaurant management, the University of Chicago for graduate studies in business, and the Haven School for the University of Miami for teaching exceptional children, he gave so that the poor could benefit from the same opportunities he had had when young.

So it was with health care. He and Corinne had available to them the best that American technology had to offer, and he wanted to help make that technology a part of the lives of others as well. Besides his involvement with La Rabida, he was on the board of Highland Park Hospital, first as trustee and then as life trustee. He made regular gifts there, funding the building of a new pediatric wing as part of the expansion program that nearly doubled the size of the hospital.

As trustee of a number of institutions, Albert made gifts, endowed scholarships, and used his business experience on budget, fund-raising, and endowment committees. The boards on which he sat gave him pleasure on many levels: he could use his expertise in ways which he knew were useful and often of long-term benefit; he made social contacts, many of which resulted in new friendships for him and Corinne; and he felt, more and more strongly as the years passed, that helping to direct the activities of institutions, especially educational, cultural, and civic ones, was the best use he could make of his time and experience. In the twenty years that spanned the '50s and '60s, he acted as advisor to Frances Roth, founder of the Culinary Institute of America, and sat on the boards of the University of Chicago, Highland Park Hospital, La Rabida Children's Hospital and Research Center, the First National

Bank of Highland Park, the Auditorium Theater Council, and the Ravinia Festival Association.

Music, of course, held a special place in his and Corinne's life. It had not always been so with Albert; Corinne later recalled concerts to which Albert dutifully accompanied her in the early years of their marriage when he worked on notes from the office during the performance or dozed off even as the tympanies were at their most vociferous. But later, with Corinne's help, he began to understand the music, to find structure and form and harmony, to hear the differences in style and ability between one performer and another; and soon he was almost as enthusiastic and critical a listener as his wife.

Their home was a center of music. Two pianos—the two that had determined the size of the living room in their new house—nestled curve to curve at one end of the long, elegant living room decorated in shades of green, white, and pumpkin. Audiences of two hundred came to concerts there, and musical guests performed alone or with Corinne. The Fine Arts Quartet, just forming in the beginning of its long, successful career, gave some of its first concerts before an audience in Corinne and Albert's living room. Corinne, herself, practiced long hours each day for her own pleasure as well as recordings and two concerts with members of the Chicago Symphony String Quartet.

In such an atmosphere, it was natural that Albert should want to use his business skills to help music flourish around Chicago. Closest to home, and almost a part of the family, was the Ravinia Festival a few blocks away. In an expansive, lush park with stately trees and shaped beds of flowers, the outdoor pavilion and indoor Murray Theater that comprised Ravinia Park were home to hundreds of thousands of music lovers each summer who picnicked on the lawn (later two restaurants were added), then stretched out on blankets and lawn chairs to hear the sound of the Chicago Symphony Orchestra and soloists on loudspeakers that carried the music throughout the park downhill from the pavilion, or moved inside to take reserved seats in the pavilion itself.

A "flashlight photo" of one of Ravinia's earliest audiences, at a concert held June 21, 1924, shows Albert, Sr., and Gertrude sitting in a front row. Albert, Jr., and Corinne probably were there that night; if not, it would have been one of the few concerts they missed. Ravinia in the summer was a fixture in their lives; and when the old wooden pavilion shown in that 1924 photo burned down, Albert was one of those who helped raise funds for a new one and the installation of an improved sound system. Over the years, his gifts continued, always for the general fund so that the Board of Trustees, the general manager, and the festival conductor could decide how best to allocate them. It was a natural step for the board to elect Albert a member, and he sat as a trustee for the rest of his life, continuing to make gifts to the festival, including a Ferrari sculpture, "Ecstasy," for the park grounds, and helping to raise other funds from individuals, corporations, and foundations. A notable contribution to the board was his formulation of the Corporate Coupon Book Sales Program, in which coupon books of twenty tickets, sold at a discount, which had always been sold to individuals in a massive campaign at the beginning of each season, were marketed to corporations to be used by them for employees or guests.

Twice, Albert was asked to serve as chairman of the Ravinia Festival Board of Trustees; he declined both times. It was uncharacteristic of him to turn down a request for such a form of help, especially in a cause in which he deeply believed. But his list of activities was long and growing longer. He was, at the time, approaching seventy; and he wanted to expand his and Corinne's travel schedule. He wanted, as he had told the *Chicago Tribune,* to be "a little more footloose."

But his interest in Ravinia never flagged; and as a trustee, he remained dedicated and active until illness forced him to cut back on all his board activity. So much a part of Ravinia's great success was he that, after his death, Emory Williams, President of the Sears Bank and a member of the Ravinia Board of Trustees, called on Corinne to tell her that the board had voted to dedicate the first piano concert of every year to Albert Pick, Jr. After her death, they added, "Corinne's name would be included in the dedication." Those piano concerts are now as firm a fixture in Ravinia's musical life as was Albert in his active, giving years.

There was another involvement with the arts, this one through the Auditorium Theater Council. The Auditorium Building—theater and hotel—had been designed by Adler and Sullivan and opened in 1889. Until 1941, the theater was a center for opera, theater, ballet, and concert recitals. (The Chicago Symphony Orchestra had played there until Orchestra Hall was built in 1904.) Albert and his family had gone there for years; at one time, an underground passage connected the Auditorium with the Congress Hotel (then called the Auditorium Hotel Annex), and parties could dine in the hotel restaurants and walk across to the opera without being buffeted by the winds that howled off Lake Michigan and down Congress street.

During the Second World War, with the Auditorium in financial trouble, the United Service Organization (USO) took it over, using the magnificent auditorium as a recreation hall; the stage was converted to bowling alleys. Maintenance ceased; after the war, the building stood empty, deteriorating in the heat of summer and the ice of winter, its grandeur barely a memory.

A remarkable woman named Beatrice Spachner led the fight to save the Auditorium. By then (1960) it was owned by Roosevelt University, housed in the entire building in which the Auditorium occupied part of the ground floor; but that institution had no money to spare for a theater, when it was trying to build a solid foundation of faculty and course offerings. Mrs. Spachner won from the university the right to "save" the Auditorium; if she found the money—which no one but she believed possible—and the university approved plans for restoration, she could form an Auditorium Council that would manage the funds and the restoration itself, as well as performances in a re-opened theater.

With the kind of persistence, doggedness, and faith that Albert most admired, she did it. And one of the first people she approached was Albert Pick, Jr., her neighbor in Highland Park and her friend. She went to his office, asked for his help as a member of the council then in formation, and asked for money. She got both. Albert joined the council, later became a member of the Executive Board, and gave money first for the restoration and then for maintenance as the theater again moved to the first ranks of Chicago's fine arts programing, this time as a not-for-profit institution. It was another of his legacies that, in 1978, a few months after his death, Mrs. Spachner, as chairperson of the Auditorium Theater Council (as she had been since its formation in 1958), and the council itself were presented with a National Trust Award for Historic Preservation.

But Albert had already paid Mrs. Spachner his own form of homage; in 1968, he gathered a group to give a bronze sculpture of Mrs. Spachner, created by Virginio Ferrari, to stand in the Auditorium; it was, he said, one way to show how they felt about Bea Spachner's "courage, persistence, and determination in the face of tremendous odds" that had led to the "restoration of a great theater, the Auditorium."

One measure of Albert's breadth of interest is a simple listing of the organizations and causes he supported, not merely with writing checks, but with time, energy, attention, thought. If education, health care, and the arts were high on his list of concerns, so was business, especially finances and the proper use of expenditures. He served on a number of committees of the National Association of Manufacturers in the 1950s, setting procedures for financial planning for both those entering the general field of manufacture and those more experienced. He served briefly, as well, on the membership committee of the U.S. Chamber of Commerce; but in 1953, his attention shifted to a new field, when Governor William Stratton appointed him to the Illinois Department of Public Welfare.

As a commissioner of the department, he was asked to supervise the regular inspections of the Elgin State Hospital (later the Elgin Mental Health Center administered by the Illinois Department of Mental Health). The mandate was not as broad, but it was similar to the one issued by the University of Chicago when Albert was asked to examine the situation at International House. There, he was given carte blanche to bring the building up to a high standard and keep it there while making it break even financially. In Elgin, he was asked, more simply, to judge the value the State was getting for the money it was spending.

He assembled a group from the hotel corporation and sent them to Elgin on a monthly basis, receiving their inspection reports and presenting them to the Department of Public Welfare. But the snarls of bureaucracy caught him; not only did he begin to feel the reports had no impact, he began to clash with other commissioners. He was in a position to see what they were doing in fields other than the one in which he was directly involved, and he found himself is disagreement with a number of them.

The most important problem, he felt, and a chronic one, was what he saw as a headlong rush to build more facilities before the department had sufficient staff to run them. He fought one project and then another, until he found himself opposing the entire building program for 1955. It was not a position he enjoyed, in large part because the "cause" was not one of those closest to him. In July, 1955, his father had died; his work with the American Hotel Association was taking more and more of his time and interest; he and Corinne were beginning to take the regular trips to Europe that would highlight their years from then on. So in 1955, he resigned from the Department of Public Welfare, ending his only venture into work with government agencies.

But he had not lost his interest (it was probably enhanced by the experience) in the effective use of money. Over the years, he had recognized his own flair for finance and the pleasure his expertise gave him. ("He was happiest," recalled psychiatrist Harold Visotsky, who knew him on the La Rabida Board of Trustees, "when he was putting together financial packages.") He was especially pleased when, in 1956, he was elected a Director of the First National Bank of Highland Park.

He knew the officers of the bank socially and through the banking he did there; he knew, as well, many of the directors who were friends and business acquaintances. Leo Sheridan of Sheridan Real Estate, Harold Florsheim, grandson of the founder and president of the Florsheim Shoe Company, and Bernard Nath of the law firm of Sonnenschein, Carlin, Nath and Rosenthal, were among the men who sat as directors and whom he admired in the professional worlds they occupied. Of all the boards on which he served, the University of Chicago and the First National Bank of Highland Park gave him the greatest sense of prestige as well as accomplishment.

Charles Kidd, who came to the bank a few years after Albert became a director, and who later was named Chairman of the Executive Committee, was one of those who not only admired his knowledge and expertise, but who cared for him personally, as well. "If I were looking for a father," he said, "I would choose Albert. He was a perfect gentleman, very soft-spoken, which I admire; and on the Executive Committee, he handled himself in such a way that convinced people to do things they might not have anticipated doing."

Albert made two marks in particular that are recalled at the bank. On the Executive Committee—that small group that makes crucial decisions for ratification by the full Board of

Directors—Albert convinced the Bank to become a "significant" rather than a token contributor to the Highland Park Hospital and to the Ravinia Festival. It was, he told them, in keeping with their role in Highland Park, a participant with other institutions in the welfare of the community. "After some time," Kidd recalled, "the bank agreed and, from then on, was a regular large contributor to both the hospital and the music festival."

More, as part of the daily activities of the bank, Albert helped formulate and codify its loan policy regarding major loans of $100,000 and up. Later, officers of large banks in downtown Chicago would say that the policy was the best of its kind they had seen for a bank the size of the First National of Highland Park. Kidd considered that another of Albert's legacies.

The busy times were good times, filled with days of blue sky and glowing sun that Albert called "large days," filled with work, filled with friends—and filled, too, with physical activity. He had not lost his love of sports since the track days of college; and in golf, especially, he found a way to relax and push his capacity. A founding member of the Northmoor Country Club in Highland Park, he won a number of golf tournaments, the most prestigious being the President's Cup, which gave him great pride, especially, as he liked to recall, since he had never had a lesson. (He was a pro sports fan, too, especially of football, which he shared with friends and with his son; he and Albert III, with three college friends, took one memorable all-male trip to the Rose Bowl in 1958 to watch Michigan State beat U.C.L.A.)

His boat, too, provided relaxation and a way to entertain; he and Corinne always took friends with them when they took trips on the yacht; the air became festive on the water. The boat was used mostly on Lake Michigan; the Eisenhowers, the Tafts, the Nixons, and a number of other political figures—local, state, and national—were guests. But most often, the guests were neighbors or those met in the course of business and travel who remained friends for twenty and thirty years.

One of their closest friends was Lawrence Kimpton. As Chancellor of the University of Chicago, he met Albert when the affiliation with La Rabida was accomplished. When Albert joined the university's Board of Trustees, he and Kimpton worked together on a number of issues. They got along well, and Marcia Kimpton and Corinne became friends when the couples began meeting at social events. When Kimpton left the university for the Standard Oil Company, there were those who said the friendship would wither, for the men were so different only the tie of the University had kept the friendship alive.

To their puzzlement, the friendship continued strong and treasured. It was not surprising in view of the breadth of Albert's interests and curiosities; there was room for so much in his days and attention that differences in personality took up less room than they might have been expected to. In any event, Albert loved and admired Kimpton as Kimpton loved him and recognized that Albert was a "complex, interesting character," as he called him in later years.

Kimpton's life was marked by tragedies, many of which Albert helped alleviate. His first wife had died before Albert met him; Marcia, his second wife, set her robe afire one evening while smoking a cigarette; and though Kimpton attempted to smother the flames and then drove frantically through the city to Billings Hospital on the campus of the University of Chicago, she died two days later.

His depression was so intense that Albert took charge. "We're going to get on the boat," he said and bundled Kimpton onto their yacht where they lived for close to three weeks, sailing the inland waterways to Florida. With no telephones, no business to conduct, no larger world to intrude, Kimpton talked and talked, of his life, of Marcia, of hopes and prayers and dreams that had died with her or with the passage of time. Albert and Corinne listened. Kimpton cooked with them in the galley, sat in the warm evening air, breathed deeply of the peace and quiet, and began to feel the wounds healing. It was a time, he said, he could not have found, with such companionship, anywhere else.

It was not his only such stay on the boat. Some time later, he married again, but within a few years death again invaded; his wife died of cancer. Kimpton recovered again on the boat; this time, to depression was added despair, a fear of fate. Still, a year later, he phoned Albert to tell of his coming marriage and to ask if he and Mary could come to dinner. "Come for a wedding," Albert said. "It will be on our front lawn." At their Miami home, then, Albert and Corinne held a wedding, with a number of guests from the University of Miami and with others who were friends of theirs and of Kimpton. And Kimpton, in the warmth of friendship, toasted Albert and Corinne for "twenty years of love."

He was not well, however. In Rome with Eleanor two years previously, joining Albert and Corinne for part of their 1967 European trip, he had become so ill that Albert had called a doctor to the hotel room. The diagnosis was emphysema and pneumonia, but Kimpton would not stay in bed nor stop smoking. Five days later he left to return to America. He recovered, but his strength was never the same. Later he had open heart surgery; he died in 1977 at the age of 67, two years after his marriage to Mary Hamilton.

Albert was told the news by Corinne; she did it with trepidation, for, by then, Albert himself was very ill, and each name that came to him of one close and dear who had died was a hammerblow on his heart. There was another who was ill: Helene Kagan, eighty-eight years old, was in a hospital in Jerusalem, and Albert worried about her. But in fact, he had been concerned about Helene for years, though for financial rather than health reasons. He and Corinne had the greatest admiration and affection for this remarkable woman, and she represented something special to both of them.

Helene Kagan, Russian Jew, medical doctor who graduated from the School of Medicine in Bern, Switzerland, with honors at the age of 24, had moved to Jerusalem in 1914. She was not allowed to practice medicine there; the Turks who ruled at the time did not allow women to take medical examinations. During the First World War, she was allowed to work as a nurse in hospitals. When a cholera epidemic broke out, and the doctors fell victim to it, she found herself in charge of a hospital for contagious diseases. She was twenty-five years old.

Her work impressed even the Turks; they granted her a doctor's license—the first woman ever to receive one from a Turkish government. There were two other Jewish doctors in Jerusalem; Helene was the only pediatrician in all Palestine. Her fame as a singular doctor and a most singular woman spread throughout the Middle East.

In 1916, she opened the first children's hospital in Jerusalem. In 1918, it was incorporated into the America Zionist Medical Unit; she headed the children's department of the hospital, General Bikur Cholim, spending much of her time on continued research into her specialty—rheumatic fever.

That was how Albert and Corinne met her. They visited General Bikur Cholim when in Israel for the International Hotel Association Congress in 1961. There had been correspondence between Bikur Cholim and La Rabida on research in rheumatic disease, and Albert was curious to see the hospital that had a reputation fine enough to cross the ocean. Helene Kagan greeted him and Corinne, took them on a tour of the hospital, and answered their questions. Her dynamism impressed them both, and they agreed later they would invite her to Chicago to visit La Rabida.

In 1963, she came, first to New York where she was Albert's guest at the Belmont Plaza Hotel. She attended pediatric society meetings, accompanied by Albert Dorfman of La Rabida who had come from Chicago for that purpose. She visited Boston and Baltimore, touring hospitals, talking to doctors, visiting with patients. Then she came to Chicago, where she stayed at the home of Albert and Corinne and spent a great deal of time at La Rabida with Dorfman.

She spoke at La Rabida to an audience of trustees, doctors, and staff from the hospital and the University of Chicago and then was honored with a plaque for more than fifty years of research and treatment of rheumatic fever and children's diseases in Palestine (Israel).

It was a good visit. Albert and Corinne were as impressed with the vitality and vibrancy of this extraordinary woman as they had been before. Since they had been in Israel in 1961, Albert had been sending money to Helene every month (she had almost none, giving all her time at low pay or in volunteer work at the hospital and with patients in her office during evening hours). Her visit confirmed Albert's feeling of her importance to Israel and to the health of children around the world; when she returned home, she took with her a pledge that the money would continue as long as she lived.

There had been other friends and acquaintances over the long, busy years—dozens, hundreds of them—but they were falling away. Joseph Caro, who had handled much of Albert's advertising through the firm of Earl Ludgin and had been a close friend, as well, died while Albert himself was in his last illness. Charles Staiger, Pauline's husband and co-sponsor with Albert of the Pick-Staiger Concert Hall at Northwestern University, died at about the same time; Corinne could not bear to tell Albert, and he died without knowing it. Roscoe ("Rocky") Miller who, as president of Northwestern University, had encouraged the building of Pick-Staiger and given Albert friendship, too, had died a short time before.

There still were many friends and many things to do, but Albert had had a warning. In 1971, as he was in the midst of negotiating his major philanthropies on university campuses, he was walking from his office to the North Western Station for the ride home to Highland Park when, almost beside his train, he blacked out and fell, his face striking the concrete platform. He was rushed to Wesley Hospital (part of the Northwestern University hospital complex in downtown Chicago), where he stayed for a week of tests for what was diagnosed as a small stroke. When he went home, the only visible signs of the incident were a black eye and a badly bruised knee.

He did not brood on the event; he knew it had been a warning, but there was so much he had to do and generally he felt very well. He was 76 years old, but he stood straight and vigorous when he walked, his eyes were clear, with a gentle smile in them that attracted so many people, and he still put in a full day at his office and at various Board meetings.

In 1972, he and Corinne, with their friends the James Van Hooks, went to Geneva for an International Hotel Association meeting. He had been told by his doctors and several friends not to go, but he felt responsible for keeping up the "American contingent" and he ignored the advice. Once there, however, he began to feel ill. Usually Europe invigorated him; both he and Corinne felt like exploring children as they discovered the nooks and crannies of Helsinki, Leningrad, Tel Aviv, Paris, Rome, Belgrade—wherever the trip of that year took them. But this time, Albert felt no inclination to go anywhere; he was weak and lethargic. He asked the organizers of the convention to let him speak first and then send him a doctor. They did both; he made his speech, on international cooperation through such organizations as People to People and professional groups both national and international, then went to his hotel room and went to bed.

Corinne had been out for the day on a tour of Geneva. When she returned and found Albert in bed, she expressed alarm. "I'm a very sick man," he said. "I've had a stroke, and I mustn't move around. They've given me medication for high blood pressure." He repeated that he was a very sick man.

She scolded him for accepting that diagnosis. Good care, rest, much love was the answer. She would see to that. They made a brief trip to England, where they were visited by George Cole, General of the British Army, whose father was a Witkowski (he had taken his wife's last name of Cole) and thus Albert, Jr.'s cousin. And when Albert regained his strength, they flew home.

It was time, they decided, to sell the business.

The times were fierce with competition and Albert knew it would take younger, stronger men to cope with the struggles of modern "innkeeping" in the corporate world that had replaced the more personal one in which he had built the company. He and Corinne thought wistfully now of the chance they had had to sell the Pick Congress; but it was too late, and they did not look back for long. Albert had a series of meetings in the Highland Park house and, when he was able, in his office downtown, but he was unable to find the kind of buyer he wanted.

By 1974, he had withdrawn from direct participation in the management of the hotel corporation. His staff, many of whom had been appointed only a short time before he became ill, was trying to cope with a complex business that required constant attention. Now there were a number of areas that were being ignored or glossed over. Albert knew it, but could not do anything about it.

It was not only the weakness that had recurred since the stroke at the Northwestern Station in 1971. He had been having trouble with his eyes, as well. It began as flashes of light that came and went but were increasing in frequency. Tested for glaucoma, he was told his eyes were normal. But it seems to have been a fluke that his eyes tested normal that day, for the flashes became worse, and he began to suffer intense pain. He and Corinne were on the way to Florida for their regular winter stay; he entered the Bascomb-Palmer Institute there for surgery in 1974.

While recovering, he asked his attorney Alan Altheimer to

handle the sale of the hotel corporation. It seemed clear to him that he would not return to it; he hoped at that time only to have health and the use of his eyes. But he was to have neither. Corinne, describing Albert in the next three years, used the metaphor of a "house of cards slowly collapsing." Her strong, vigorous, handsome, and beloved husband became weaker with each day; his eyes did not improve with surgery but deteriorated to the point that he could see only shadows and the strong concentrated light of a television screen. He became angry at his helplessness, and the fury raging within him contributed to a severe depression. His mind, as keen as ever, raced with memories and unfulfilled plans—some he talked over with Corinne; others he kept within himself with a growing sense of despair.

He had visits from friends and, best of all, from the grandchildren he adored. But he was impatient; there was no progress, he felt, in his vision or his health. He had had a series of small strokes that had left him nearly an invalid; and in 1977, he asked to be admitted to Billings Hospital at the University of Chicago, where he knew a number of doctors whose judgment and skill he trusted. The ambulance that took him to the hospital raced, and Albert asked the attendant why they couldn't slow down. A pregnant woman needed the ambulance next, he was told. She had gone into labor early. Albert smiled a small shadow of his former broad grin. "You should have told her to give one good push," he said. "Then she wouldn't have needed an ambulance at all."

But he drew on his own humor less and less. He lay in the hospital bed, "holding court," as friends, doctors, and staff members came to call; there was an outpouring of friendship and affection that he would have appreciated more if he had not been so weary.

In November, Chauncey Harris, Director of the School of International Studies at Pick Hall of the University of Chicago, and John Wilson, acting Chancellor of the University, visited him in his room. He told them he wanted to make sure the scholarship he was establishing in Lawrence Kimpton's name was complete, with all the paper work done. Harris drafted a letter of acceptance of the scholarship, and John Wilson signed it, with copies for Albert and his secretary, Nadine Van Sant. With that accomplished, Albert sank back into his pillows and, in a quiet voice, spoke of his years in Chicago and his relations with the University of Chicago. Harris later recalled the "summary" tone of what he said; he was reviewing years of thoughts, observations, activities, and business and social relationships in a way that placed them all in a framework of a long, full life. He became very tired, his voice sometimes fading to a whisper; but he talked for almost an hour, closing with the scholarship he had just established in the name of one of his closest friends who had been affiliated with one of the insituations to which Albert felt most bound. Harris felt he was closing the book on his own life. Then he fell silent, his eyes closed, and Corinne said it was time for him to rest. Harris and Wilson left; it was the last time they saw him.

A week later, he underwent cataract surgery which restored the vision in one of his eyes; but he had only two days to feel he might yet, as he told Corinne, "join you on the golf course this winter." In the evening of December 10, he had a heart attack and lay in a coma for some hours. Corinne was called to his room from the apartment near the hospital where she had moved for the duration of his stay; he regained consciousness sufficiently to know she was there, but he never knew that Albert III and his wife were there as well. He died in the early morning hours of December 11, 1977.

❡

As honors had come to him during his lifetime, they came after his death.

The eulogy at his funeral was delivered by Preston Bradley, who had told him "we love you" at his and Corinne's fiftieth wedding celebration. Bradley talked of the measure of a man and the space he occupied in life and quoted from the Talmud: "The greatest boon of all when one leaves this world is to be able to wear the indestructible crown of a good name."

Letters came to Corinne—over eight hundred in all—from around the world, expressing affection and sorrow. Many announced scholarships in Albert's name or gifts to a number of causes. The University of Chicago Board of Trustees passed a resolution honoring him and his service to education, in general, and the university, in particular.

At Northwestern University, a memorial concert was held in Pick-Staiger Hall on May 14, 1978. The Symphonic Wind Ensemble, piano, organ, and chorus joined in a program that concluded with Franz Schubert's Mass in F, the *Deutsche Masse*. The program was presented by the Northwestern University Music Society, of which Corinne was an honorary life member; the program notes opened with a statement by Thomas V. Miller, Dean of the School of Music, who wrote:

> Albert Pick had a dream that this concert hall would be among the best. To ensure this, he invited his brother-in-law, Charles Staiger, to join him in this project to honor two very special women, Corinne Frada Pick and Pauline Pick Staiger. It is a credit to their interest and commitment that Pick-Staiger Concert Hall has been so fully realized in the beauty of its setting, its interiors, and its acoustics.
>
> Not only does the Pick-Staiger Concert Hall benefit Northwestern University, but also it exists in a wider frame of reference. A university, in addition to its function as a community of scholars, serves as a gathering of witnesses to excellence.

Of all that could be said of Albert Pick, Jr., that phrase probably is the one he most would have clasped as a legacy: that in his life and work, in the marriage he made with Corinne, in his friendships and philanthropies, he had contributed to a gathering of witnesses to excellence.

Index